THE DOCTORS BOOK
OF
Home
Remedies®
FOR
SHARPER
MEMORY

Titles in
The Doctors Book of Home Remedies
series

THE DOCTORS BOOK
OF
Home Remedies®
FOR
SHARPER MEMORY

Learn More Than 100 All-New Techniques from America's Top Memory Experts

By the Editors of *PREVENTION*.
Edited by Mary S. Kittel

RODALE

Cover Designers: Christina Gaugler, Tara Long

Library of Congress Cataloging-in-Publication Data

The doctors book of home remedies for sharper memory /
  by the editors of Prevention ; edited by Mary S. Kittel.
      p.   cm.
  Includes index.
  ISBN 1–57954–233–6 paperback
  1. Mnemonics. 2. Memory. I. Kittel, Mary S.
II. Prevention (Emmaus, Pa.)
BF385 .D63 2000
153.1'2—dc21   00–036602

Distributed to the book trade by St. Martin's Press

2 4 6 8 10 9 7 5 3 1 paperback

Visit us on the Web at www.rodaleremedies.com,
or call us toll-free at (800) 848-4735.

WE **INSPIRE** AND **ENABLE** PEOPLE TO IMPROVE
THEIR LIVES AND THE WORLD AROUND THEM

About *Prevention* Health Books

The editors of *Prevention* Health Books are dedicated to providing you with authoritative, trustworthy, and innovative advice for a healthy, active lifestyle. In all of our books, our goal is to keep you thoroughly informed about the latest breakthroughs in natural healing, medical research, alternative health, herbs, nutrition, fitness, and weight loss. We cut through the confusion of today's conflicting health reports to deliver clear, concise, and definitive health information that you can trust. And we explain in practical terms what each new breakthrough means to you, so you can take immediate, practical steps to improve your health and well-being.

Every recommendation in *Prevention* Health Books is based upon interviews with highly qualified health authorities, including medical doctors and practitioners of alternative medicine. In addition, we consult with the *Prevention* Health Books Board of Advisors to ensure that all of the health information is safe, practical, and up-to-date. *Prevention* Health Books are thoroughly factchecked for accuracy, and we make every effort to verify recommendations, dosages, and cautions.

The advice in this book will help keep you well-informed about your personal choices in health care—to help you lead a happier, healthier, and longer life.

Notice

This book is intended as a reference volume only, not as a medical manual. The information given here is designed to help you make informed decisions about your health. It is not intended as a substitute for any treatment that may have been prescribed by your doctor. If you suspect that you have a medical problem, we urge you to seek competent medical help.

Acknowledgments

Writers: Barbara Boughton, Karen Cicero, John Forester, Brian Good, Dana Sullivan, Elizabeth Torg, Mariska van Aalst
Editorial Researcher: Jennifer Kushnier
Contributing Editor: Doug Dollemore

We would like to thank the following health care professionals for their contributions to this book:
Elaine Andrews; Tora Brawley, Ph.D.; Alan S. Brown, Ph.D.; Ann B. Bruner, M.D.; Cole Burrell; Antonio Capurso, M.D.; Michael Chafetz, Ph.D.; Stephen Chew, Ph.D.; Irene Colsky, Ed.D.; Thomas Crook III, Ph.D.; Charles DeCarli, M.D.; Victor Davich; Wolfgang Ellermeier, Ph.D.; Michael Epstein, Ph.D., D.Ph.; Larry J. Feldman, Ph.D.; Trisha Lamb Feuerstein; Michelle Filoia; Robert Finkel, Ph.D.; Janet Fogler; William F. Fry, M.D.; Scott Gerson, M.D.; Dennis Gersten, M.D.; Barry Gordon, M.D., Ph.D.; Jordan Grafman, Ph.D.; Murray Grossman, M.D., Ph.D.; Carla Hannaford, Ph.D; Douglas Herrmann, Ph.D.; Robert Houde; Siu Lui Hui, Ph.D.; James Joseph, Ph.D.; Robin Kanarek, Ph.D.; Lawrence C. Katz, Ph.D.; Susan Kavaler-Adler, Ph.D.; Alan D. Kozikowski, Ph.D.; Arthur F. Kramer, Ph.D.; Joshua Landau, Ph.D.; Danielle Lapp; Asenath LaRue, Ph.D.; Harry Lorayne; Vernon Mark, M.D.; Mark Mattson, Ph.D.; Sam Migdole, Ed.D.; Richard Mohs, Ph.D.; David Molony, L.Ac.; Ming Ming Pan Molony, O.M.D.; Roger von Oech; Barry Oken, M.D.; Snowdon Parlette, Ph.D.; James Penland, Ph.D.; Francis Pirozzolo, M.D.; W. Stephen Pray, Ph.D., R.Ph.; Michael Pressley, Ph.D.; Ed Reibscheid; Arnold B. Scheibel, M.D.; Alan Searleman, Ph.D.; Joyce Simard; Maria Simonson, Ph.D.; Lynn Smaha, M.D.; Mark Stengler, N.D.; James Swan, Ph.D.; Scott Terry, Ph.D.; Connie Tomaino, D.A.; Katherine Tucker, Ph.D.; Roy Upton, AHG; Charles A. Weaver III, Ph.D.; Julian Whitaker, M.D.; Mark Williams, M.D.; Sherry Willis, Ph.D.; Arthur Winter, M.D.; Richard Saul Wurman

Contents

MENTAL NUTRIENTS

Read about a soy extract that can improve IQ, vitamins that increase brain activity, and foods that can feed your mind. Nutritionists and neurologists offer diet advice and tips for taking incredible memory-boosting herbs, vitamins, minerals, and other research-proven supplements.

SMART MOVES

Tuning up your physical and emotional wellness is essential for maximum mental health. Strategies that can truly make the difference between cloudy and sharp thinking include getting sounder sleep, socializing, sports, laughter, meditation, and avoiding the blues.

ALTERNATIVE OPTIONS

A nontraditional healer may offer just the right help to remove your mental blocks. This chapter introduces you to hypnotists, meditation teachers, acupuncturists, herbalists, Oriental doctors, and more.

INDEX

Use It, Don't Lose It

Just before a concert, a clarinetist woefully approached the great Italian conductor Arturo Toscanini and said that he would be unable to perform since his instrument was broken and he couldn't play E-natural. Toscanini thought deeply for a long moment, mentally sorting through the thousands of notes that would be played that evening. Finally, the maestro announced, "It's all right. You don't have an E-natural tonight."

Even in his eighties, Toscanini could easily recall great volumes of music. That may seem extraordinary, but experts say that stupendous memory isn't just for the young. The latest word on the brain power front is that virtually every one of us can maintain sharp, crystal-clear recall for the rest of our lives because of one underappreciated fact: Significant memory loss is *not* an inevitable part of aging. In fact, all it may take to keep your memory in peak condition is plenty of mental stimulation, regular exercise, some dietary adjustments, patience, and perhaps a few memorization tricks to tweak your mind at key moments.

Your A-maze-ing Mind

In many ways, the brain is a maze through which scientists are still trying to wend their way. But researchers do know a lot about how memories are formed. It helps to know a bit of Brain Matter 101.

Within your brain are billions of nerve cells called neurons. These cells communicate with each other by releasing chemicals called neurotransmitters. These chemicals are released from a cell through axons and received by dendrites, both of which are rootlike structures that branch out and seek connections with adjoining cells. The more of these connections you have between your cells, the greater your brain power.

In simple terms, a memory is a recording. The neurons are the tape that memory is recorded on, and a region of the brain called the hippocampus is what turns the mind's tape recorder on and off. Most of the time, the recorder is turned off. So a lot of information that is only momentarily important, such as a new telephone number or the name of the person you sat next to on a plane, zips quickly out of your mind. But if your brain considers something worth remembering, the hippocampus starts the recording process, and neurons begin forming connections that will permanently store the information in various locations in your brain. It can take millions of neurons to form a single memory.

"It's like looking at your television. If you look very carefully, you'll notice that the television picture is made up of little dots. It's the pattern of those dots that form the picture. The neurons are forming similar patterns in your brain to form a memory," says Barry Gordon, M.D., Ph.D., a behavioral neurologist at the Johns Hopkins School of Medicine in Baltimore and author of *Memory: Remembering and Forgetting in Everyday Life*.

Watch Out for These Brain Drainers

Of course, like any recording device, the brain has glitches. That's why memory is far from perfect at any age. Everyone misplaces keys or pocketbooks, or forgets appointments occasionally. It happens; it's just a part of life. But beginning at about age 45, it does take longer to recall things. As we age, we also need more time and effort to process new information. By age 64, many people develop what is known as tip-of-the-tongue phenomenon—difficulty remembering a common, once-familiar word. As you get older, you may have trouble recalling lists, directions, or even dreams.

Usually, these changes are mere annoyances and seldom signal that your brain is turning to mush. No one is certain why these changes occur, but some researchers suspect that changes in hearing, vision, and other senses impair the brain's ability to collect and store memories. Emotional upheavals, such as stress and depression, can affect your memory as well. Medications such as over-the-counter cold remedies and sleeping pills dampen recollection. Information overload and hectic lifestyles may also compound the problem.

"One reason people think they have such poor memories is that they are trying to do too much too quickly," says Arthur Kramer, Ph.D., professor of psychology at the Beckman Institute at the University of Illinois at Urbana–Champaign. "We know that if you try to memorize something and you try to do something else simultaneously, it doesn't work very well. And I think we're always trying to do that. We simply don't give ourselves the time to remember well."

Then there are hormones. Estrogen in particular appears to play a role in some memory functions. Research from McGill University in Quebec found that postmenopausal women who took estrogen scored higher on recall tests than postmenopausal women who did not take estrogen.

Nutritional deficiencies also can trigger memory problems. People who live alone, particularly older individuals, may not eat often or well, and that can have a tremendous impact on thinking and recollection.

Recoup Your Losses

As we get older, the brain does shrink a bit. But contrary to popular belief, we really don't lose many brain cells as we age. We're born with about 100 billion brain cells, and at age 100, most people still have 96.35 billion.

There is other exciting news about the brain. Until recently, researchers believed that we had a finite number of brain cells because—unlike other cells in the body—brain cells could not reproduce. But in the past few years, scientists have discovered a source, close to the base of the brain, called the subventricular region, where new, immature cells are continuously being generated, says Arnold B. Scheibel, M.D., professor of neurobiology and psychology at the University of California, Los Angeles. These cells can migrate throughout the brain to areas where they can take up roles that enhance the inner workings of your mind.

So breakthrough research is showing that your brain does indeed produce fresh neurons over time. And even though these new cells apparently don't replace all of the neurons that die off, many of the remaining brain cells branch out to form new connections in the brain. These new connections, combined with the growth of new neurons, help keep your memories intact and your brain sharp.

Take Charge

Despite its many challenges, your brain is a marvelous structure capable of extraordinary feats of recall even late in life. For the vast majority of us, the fear of slipping away into a shroud of faulty memory and dementia over time is unfounded, according to Mark Williams, M.D., author of *The American Geriatrics Society's Complete Guide to Aging and Health*.

In fact, there are plenty of things you can do to maintain

your current memory capacity, fend off any potential future declines, and even *boost* your powers of recall at any age. With this book in hand, you have all of the tools you'll need. Here's an overview of what you'll find.

A certain smell triggers memories of days spent at Grandma's house. A particular song brings back the details of your college days. Most of us can think of examples in which our senses—sight, smell, hearing, taste, and touch—are linked with powerful pictures from the past. Extrasensory Skills looks at how to tap these same senses as a means to enhance your recall power. We'll show you how surrounding yourself with certain colors and scents can work to your mind's advantage and how other sensory experiences, such as massage and music, can do wonders, too.

Mind Games shows you how a host of tricks, from rhyming to repetition, can strengthen the connections between neurons in your brain and help you boost your memory skills.

Just as diet and nutrition plays a role with so many other aspects of your health and well-being, so it goes with memory too. In Mental Nutrients, you'll learn about the memory-enhancing capacity of B vitamins, the role of "mind" minerals, and plenty of new findings about herbs and supplements that you can use for memory enhancement.

If you've tried a dozen brain games and are ready for a real change of pace, double-time it to Smart Moves. There, you'll find the lowdown on how aerobic exercises such as walking, jogging, and swimming as well as meditation and even regular social interaction can boost your concentration and make you a sharper, more intellectually alert adult.

Finally, if nontraditional healing methods appeal to you, check out Alternative Options. Here you'll find tips and advice from hypnotists and an assortment of holistic healers.

When to See the Doctor

More than 70 conditions can trigger or worsen memory difficulties, including hearing loss, vision problems, thyroid conditions, high blood pressure, and depression. Many of these problems are treatable or even reversible, so see your doctor if any of the following apply to you.

- You frequently get lost while driving a familiar route.
- You often forget important appointments.
- You tell the same story over and over to the same person in a single conversation.
- You find yourself unable to manage simple problems—like balancing a checkbook—that you have always done with ease in the past.
- You experience a personality change.
- You have language difficulty like being unable to name a common object like a knife, spoon, or fork.
- You have periods when you are confused about the time of day or where you are.
- You notice a sudden change in your artistic or musical abilities.

Extrasensory Skills

"Memory is a magnet. It will pull to it and hold only material nature has designed it to attract."

—Jessamyn West, *U.S. author*

FOLLOW YOUR SENSES TO BETTER ATTENTION

The first step you must take when you want to improve your memory skills is to make sure the information gets to your memory in the first place.

According to Michael L. Epstein, Ph.D., D.Ph., information has to overcome three hurdles before getting into your memory. The first hurdle is a sensory buffer. You have to see, hear, touch, smell or otherwise experience through a combination of the senses the information you want to remember. After that, you have to get that information into the short-term memory zone, where it is processed and either discarded or sent on to the third hurdle, the long-term memory.

But to make it over the first hurdle, you have to be engaged in what you're experiencing by being aware of what your senses are taking in. Think of all the times you have trouble remembering directions or names because you weren't really paying attention when you first heard them. Instead, maybe you were thinking of a recent argument, or planning when to pick up the dry cleaning. "We are often so worried about what we are going to say or do next that the moment at hand never gets into our short-term memory," says Dr. Epstein.

You never know when a conversation or an experience is going to be important to reference later on, so make a habit out of being alert and interested in what is happening at the present moment. Do this by allowing yourself to fully hear, smell, see, and feel your surroundings. By staying focused through your senses, important information will make it past that first hurdle. And the more you're engaged, the less you'll catch yourself being absentminded, not to mention bored—even during that next budget meeting.

—Michael L. Epstein, Ph.D., D.Ph., *is a professor of psychology at Rider University in Lawrenceville, New Jersey, who specializes in memory research.*

LISTEN AND LEARN

Listening to certain music can affect your long-term memory, your critical thinking skills, and even the speed of your thoughts.

Music has long been a part of worship, teaching, story-telling, and advertising—all disciplines in which memory is key.

Now, music has found its way into the medical world. Researchers have discovered that some music will actually cause your neurons to fire at faster or slower rates. The greater the number of rhythmic beats, the higher the level of brain activity, explains music therapist Connie Tomaino, D.A. Many music therapists and other healers believe that different sounds and various instruments affect specific organs and organ systems in the physical body and are able to break blockages in energy flow.

At popular bookstores and record shops, you can purchase music engineered by scientists in the field of "psychoacoustics"—the study of sound on consciousness. Try listening, for example, to Dr. Andrew Weil's *Sound Body, Sound Mind* while reading or writing letters to take advantage of your brain's heightened power.

When approached critically, music can sharpen your complex thinking skills. "You can develop the analytical side of your brain by studying a piece of jazz or classical music," says Dr. Tomaino. "Try to identify the various instruments, think about tempo, phrasing, and mood. You'll get more adept as you spend more time with each piece," she adds.

—Connie Tomaino, D.A., *a doctor of arts in music therapy, is the director of music therapy at Beth Abraham Health Services in the Bronx, New York.*

KEEP A SENSE DIARY

You log your checks and credit card payments. Why not write down the things you really want to remember? You'll benefit for years to come.

Whether you are writing a mystery novel or just making a one-paragraph entry in your daily journal, you are helping to keep your mind sharp. Because you focus on recollecting one thought at a time, word by word, journal writing helps you clarify your thoughts, engage your memory, and improve your logical thinking skills.

Journal writing is an excellent tool to cut through your mental chatter. But one of the hardest things about keeping a journal is figuring out where to start writing, says Susan Kavaler-Adler, Ph.D. Using one of your senses as a topic can give you a place to begin, while also preserving whatever sensory experience you are describing. Senses are the way we first filter all experience, so by concentrating on that sense, you may have a direct line back to a specific memory.

Start on Monday by describing an experience about your sense of smell; on Tuesday describe taste, Wednesday describe touch, and so on. Let the sense be your entry into your writing. Once you describe one sensory memory experience, you'll be able to make quick associations with other memories.

Let's say that next Monday your "assignment" is smell, and you think about the scent of roses. Suddenly, you're back in time, playing in your grandmother's garden in late summer, surrounded by the brash torrent of pink and red roses spilling down from the trellis, feeling the bush's thorns and sticky leaves. With all these sense memories flooding back, you won't be able to stop writing!

By starting your writing session with material as rich and easy to describe as a sensory experience, you should also be short-circuiting what Dr. Kavaler-Adler calls the internal editor, a critical inner voice that often stifles creative expression. But if you do get stuck, move on to another sense. The key is to keep going.

—Susan Kavaler-Adler, Ph.D., *a psychologist in Manhattan, is the founding director of the Object Relations Institute for Psychotherapy and Psychoanalysis, author of* The Compulsion to Create, *and leader of ongoing writing groups.*

TUNE UP YOUR BRAIN

Learn to play an instrument. You'll entertain yourself and your friends, and you'll boost your brain power to boot.

Playing music is the ultimate brain cross-training. With it, you develop motor skills, identify the musical notes, and pair those symbols with sounds, while focusing your mind on attentive listening. "All these cognitive skills are happening simultaneously, so you're really challenging yourself," says music therapist Connie Tomaino, D.A.

The best part about music? You can learn to play at any age. Decide what kind of music you love and let that passion help you choose your instrument.

Ideally, Dr. Tomaino says, you should practice for at least 10 to 15 minutes every day to nail the basics, then start practicing longer as you move on to more challenging music-making. If you play only once a week, you'll get stuck at ground zero—creating just another routine and negating all the good you're trying to do for your brain.

Once you master the basics, you can learn new pieces of music, play in an ensemble, and even memorize the music. "As each skill is mastered, it's processed by a different part of the brain and becomes a reflex skill," says Dr. Tomaino. "Your brain then goes on autopilot and uses your attention to learn new skills." So the important thing is to keep reaching for new levels, she says.

—Connie Tomaino, D.A., *a doctor of arts in music therapy, is the director of music therapy at Beth Abraham Health Services in the Bronx, New York.*

DRAW STRENGTH FROM WEAKNESS

Using your nondominant hand to open the door to your house might unlock a stifled memory.

Have you ever tried to write your signature with your nondominant hand? Remember how hard you had to focus to get even your first name down on the page? By struggling through an activity that normally comes very easily to you, you are activating underused pathways in your brain that are just waiting to be tapped, says Lawrence C. Katz, Ph.D.

Pick any activity that you naturally do with one hand or the other: brushing your teeth, buttoning a shirt, tying your shoes, dealing cards. When you do it with the opposite hand, the brain registers the immediate contrast to your normal modus operandi. Opposing brain hemispheres, normally unchallenged when doing this task, are activated by the sensory and motor information sent by that different hand or foot—which means major gains in brain circuit development.

Try to incorporate several nondominant-hand tasks into your daily habits. "Like any lifestyle change, you may not feel immediate results, but they will gradually accrue over time," says Dr. Katz.

Naturally, though, this challenge is just for risk-free tasks. "I'd be a little cautious about using your nondominant hand for certain things," Dr. Katz warns. "You don't want to cut steaks or use power tools or chain saws."

—Lawrence C. Katz, Ph.D., *is a professor of neurobiology at Duke University and coauthor of* Keep Your Brain Alive.

MASSAGE REJUVENATES BODY AND MIND

It's more than a luxurious extravagance; massage could make you smarter!

Massage is a fantastic remedy for stress relief, but don't underestimate the benefits for your memory. Massage can excite your brain into better functioning, says Larry J. Feldman, Ph.D.

Scientists theorize that just the act of being touched increases production of a hormone within the brain called Nerve Growth Factor (NGF). This hormone encourages new brain cell development and helps produce neurotransmitters that affect memory and learning.

Although the NGF theory has yet to be proven, what is known for certain is that massage helps to stimulate the lymphatic system, which supplies oxygen-rich liquid to the cells, keeping your brain cells healthy, says Dr. Feldman.

Luckily, you don't need to rely on a willing spouse or a highly paid masseuse to give you this healthy touch. Dr. Feldman recommends trying these self-massage techniques when you're taking a quick break at your desk or while you're stuck in traffic.

1. Place the pads of four fingertips together at the center of your forehead. Very gently, smooth along the "worry" lines of your forehead from the center out to the temples. Repeat six times.

2. Using pressure no harder than the touch you would use on your eyeball, make tiny circles on your temples, between the corner of your eye and your scalp. Repeat six times.

3. Using slightly firmer pressure with all of your fingers, massage your scalp with circular motions. Starting at the nape of your neck, work your fingers around until you have massaged each part of your scalp. As you massage, imagine that your scalp is loosening under your touch.

4. Make a loose fist close to the scalp and grab a handful of hair close to the scalp. Give your hair a little tug. Repeat, grabbing more clumps of hair, until you've covered each section of the scalp.

—Larry J. Feldman, Ph.D., *is the director of the Pain and Stress Rehabilitation Center in New Castle, Delaware.*

USE AROMATHERAPY TO ACTIVATE YOUR MIND

Just a quick sniff of rosemary or basil might give you the extra edge that can earn you an A+ memory.

Brain wave tests show that inhaling the scents of rosemary and basil increase beta waves that indicate a state of heightened awareness in the brain. Keep these scents in mind when it comes to taking tests or when you're in other situations requiring high brain performance.

Healers have used these herbs as nervous system stimulants for hundreds of years. If one of aromatherapist Elaine Andrews' clients wants to boost her brain power or memory, Andrews uses rosemary or basil in a diffuser while she's giving them a facial. Or she puts the essential oil in a neutral base oil and uses the mixture for a massage.

A major appeal of aromatherapy is its portability—you can easily take advantage of its potent power during a test or speech. When studying or preparing, put some rosemary or basil oil in a diffuser in the room with you. On performance day, put just a trace of essential oil of that herb in your hair or on a handkerchief. Not only are rosemary and basil potent brain boosters, but the familiar scent helps to flash you back to when you took in the information. And according to psychologists, you're more likely to recall information in the same atmosphere in which you learned it.

Of course, you don't always want to think at 90 miles an hour. Because they can be such potent stimulants, Andrews advises you to avoid using rosemary and basil after 6:00 P.M.

—Elaine Andrews *is an aromatherapist and the owner of Paradise Day Spa in San Diego.*

LET THE EARTH RECHARGE YOU

Seeking out and visiting a special spot in nature can improve your memory by helping you to increase your focus, to relax, and to sharpen your observational skills.

"One issue with memory is divided attention," says environmental psychologist James Swan, Ph.D. "If you take time in nature to 'recharge your batteries,' you will feel clearer and your memory is likely to increase."

Find a spot in nature that you connect with, says Dr.

Swan, preferably within walking distance of your home or work. The spot you choose could be on a rock near a lake, in a small stand of woods, or even in a quiet park. Try to spend at least a half-hour there once a week, and don't take anything that might distract you, such as a book or a personal stereo.

Let your senses deliver messages to you by using "soft eyes," not focusing too strongly on any one element. Think about how your perceptions sharpen as you spend more time in your spot: Do you notice the sweetness of honeysuckle, the color of sunlight through leaves, or the harmony of singing birds?

"Emotional 'old business' will fade away and you will become more focused and alert," says Dr. Swan. "Memory is tied into being grounded and centered and living in your body. Immersion in nature helps to create a profound sense of balance and physical awareness."

—James Swan, Ph.D., *is an environmental psychologist in Mill Valley, California, and the author of* Nature as Teacher and Healer.

GET OUT OF TOWN— AND GET SMART

Educational travel uses all of your senses to expand your knowledge of other cultures and places, making the world your multidimensional classroom.

According to memory experts, the more senses you involve in the learning process, the more likely you are to absorb information. Travel allows you to experience and learn with all five senses simultaneously.

In fact, neurologists say that a constant barrage of novel information—such as the kind travel offers—will stimulate new dendrite connections that increase communication among brain cells.

Whether you're floating down the Grand Canal in Venice or listening to an Irish ballad in a Dublin pub, your varied sensual experiences will help reinforce the country's culture, art, language, and history. In other words, you're actively learning new information—with all of your senses engaged in the learning process.

"The idea behind educational travel is more than seeing the countries and buildings—it's to learn while you do it," says travel expert Ed Reibscheid. Think of an educational tour or program as a classroom that opens its doors to the world. It's interesting to study the history of Turkey, for instance, but it's much more stimulating to walk through a market in Istanbul, hear the offers for tarragon and saffron called out in Turkish, smell the overflowing barrels of coffee and olives, and touch the fine workmanship of a handmade rug while you make your way toward the visual splendor of the famous Blue Mosque.

The smell, touch, taste, sound, and sight of your first-hand experience will help you remember your vacation, boost your brain power, and gain a broader perspective on life for years to come.

—Ed Reibscheid *is the director of production and marketing for Thomas P. Gohagan & Company, a Chicago travel agency that organizes alumni and group tours.*

BECOME AN ART CRITIC

Head to your local art museum to reap brain-boosting rewards.

Research suggests that browsing among art may slow the cognitive decline that comes with aging. That's because the process of appreciating art calls so many different thinking skills into use, says Joshua Landau, Ph.D.

When you look at a piece of art, you challenge your memory to formulate an impression based on past knowledge. Your mind scans the various media that it knows and identifies the genre of the work. You may remember styles from a long-ago art appreciation course or from a book you read last week. Putting together all of the ideas that you recall and that you observe, you may be able to come to some definite conclusions about the style and school of the work while also clarifying your own opinions.

Each time you stimulate your brain this way, your neurons reach out to each other with dendrites, new connections that reinforce learning and keep your brain strong.

And don't be disdainful if you never make it to the Louvre. Viewing the work of local artists exhibited in your neighborhood art center is just as beneficial. "The content is not as important as the amount of thinking you do and the intellectual connections you make while you are in the museum," says Dr. Landau.

—Joshua Landau, Ph.D., *is an assistant professor of behavioral sciences at York College of Pennsylvania.*

DESIGN A BRAIN-BOOSTING GARDEN

Before your first marigold springs from the earth, you'll already have used many mental skills that are key to preventing memory decline with age.

Planning and planting your garden can be both a university and a spa for your brain. Planning a garden involves studying plants' names and thinking about their seasons, soil needs, textures, and colors, and remembering how those plants fared during last year's drought or frost. On a larger scale, planning also requires abstract spatial thinking. And because spatial memory is susceptible to decline as we age, giving it a little extra workout is especially important, according to neurologists.

While visualizing your garden, you're considering how a plant will take up and leave space and how it will interact with the other plants, trees, beds, fences, and walls around it. If you sketch out your ideas and commit your plan to paper, you'll be further flexing your spatial relationship skills while reinforcing exactly where you wanted that holly tree.

Need some ideas? Begin your plan by sitting in your friends' gardens, taking community garden tours, or wandering in botanical gardens, suggests landscape designer Cole Burrell. Consider how all of the design elements work together. Why were certain shrubs, trees, walls, structures, grasses, and flowers selected? Do flat or raised beds appeal to you? What kinds of shapes do the different groups of plants make? Notice what textures you like for mulching and walkways, such as pine needles, stones, or ground-up tires.

Analyze the design of the garden by taking photos or sketching the different sections and thinking of how each contributes to the overall plan. "If you can learn to see spatial relationships and to reproduce them, rather than just thinking, 'Isn't that pretty?' you're halfway to being able to produce the same effect yourself," says Burrell.

Once your plan is put into action, your brain will be treated to a stimulating feast of color and light as well as benefiting from the spatial thinking you exerted.

—Cole Burrell *is a native landscape designer in Free Union, Virginia, and author of* A Gardener's Encyclopedia of Wildflowers.

EXCITE YOUR BRAIN WITH NATURE'S PALETTE

Enjoying a vast array of vivid garden colors will excite your brain into new levels of activity.

The more color and the more texture your garden has— and the more you take advantage of it by spending time in your creation—the more stimulating it will be to the brain," says Maria Simonson, Ph.D.

The brain benefits of gardening don't end with the challenges of planning and planting. The sensory experience of enjoying the fruits of your labors can be nourishing to your mind. Perhaps the most beneficial of gardening pleasures is the sight of your flower beds' colorful interplay.

Memory experts say that warm garden colors like reds, oranges, deep yellows, vibrant purples, and magentas are more visually and mentally stimulating than cool colors because they play off the light of the sun or the shade of the shadows. Strong color contrasts like blue and orange also offer a high level of stimulation.

"Yellow is the first color you'll notice," says Dr. Simonson. "It can lift your spirits and make you feel happy and optimistic." The color red has been shown to raise blood pressure, respiration, heart rate, and brain waves—so consider the power of a bed of roses or poppies in full bloom! For best effect, mix yellow and red for an energizing combination.

—Maria Simonson, Ph.D., *is the director of the Health, Weight, and Stress Clinic of Johns Hopkins Medical Institutions in Baltimore.*

APPRECIATE WINE TO GET SMART

Wine's properties are good for your heart, but wine's pleasures are good for your head.

An appreciation of wine can help you improve critical thinking skills, your verbal ability, and your overall knowledge base. Not to mention that wine-tasting can add significant flair to your social life!

When you first look at a glass of wine, you're exercising your visual and recollection skills by comparing the color and clarity to other wines you've known before. Then you smell the wine, which is actually 90 percent of tasting it. "The taste is described in terms of sweetness, saltiness, bitterness, or sourness," says Robert Houde, sommelier with Charlie Trotter's, a restaurant in Chicago that carries 1,200 wines. "When it comes to tasting, you think about how to put these sensations into words."

To start tasting wine, Houde recommends choosing a single variety of wine, such as cabernet, and getting a group of friends together to compare different vineyards' products. You can use a wine source book, like *Wine Spectator's Ultimate Guide to Buying Wine* to give you some basics, but the most important thing is to have fun. Doctors say that you retain information much better when you enjoy what you're doing because when you feel emotion, you produce norepinephrine, a neurotransmitter that helps your brain solidify your experience in long-term memory.

Every time you taste a new wine, your palate will become more sophisticated. Tasting an exceptional wine (what Houde calls a barometer) can help you develop a natural evaluation system and create a series of relationships among wines. Over time, these mental connections will consolidate into a hobby with a rich body of knowledge that you can expand upon for the rest of your life—a factor that doctors say is very important in the brain's continued resilience and growth.

Just don't overdo it. Overconsumption of alcohol impedes new learning, and alcohol abuse can cause brain damage. Although studies show that drinking one glass of wine can improve blood flow to the brain, doctors say that drinking to the point of tipsiness is linked to memory loss.

—Robert Houde *is sommelier for the 1,200 wines served at Charlie Trotter's in Chicago.*

ELIMINATE
NOISE POLLUTION

A white noise machine may improve your ability to remember by drowning out distractions.

It's a familiar scene: You're trying to remember someone's phone number, when your kids tear around the corner screaming your name, the dog starts barking, and suddenly the string of numbers evaporates into the ether. It's not so bad if it's an isolated occurrence, but if you're studying for a test or a major presentation, the interference can be maddening.

"Background speech can really disrupt memory—no matter if the sound is delivered at the level of a whisper or a shout," says Wolfgang Ellermeier, Ph.D. Unfortunately, ear plugs probably won't help you, says Dr. Ellermeier, since they've been designed to muffle industrial noise yet still allow you to detect speech.

Instead, he proposes trying a white noise machine, a small device the size of a clock radio, which is often successful at drowning out speech and music. The machine emits a subtle static sound known as white noise, made up of sound waves of all frequencies in the audio spectrum. You can purchase a white noise machine through a number of electronics suppliers.

Provided the white noise itself does not become annoying, Dr. Ellermeier says that the reduction of aural distractions might help you seal the information you want into your memory.

—Wolfgang Ellermeier, Ph.D., *is associate professor and the head of the auditory perception laboratory at the Institute for Psychology at the University of Regensburg in Germany.*

MIX UP YOUR MIND

Just about any habit can get a bit mind-numbing. In order to keep your wits sharp, it's crucial to shake up your brain a little bit.

You don't have to quit your job every year or move across the country to get the change of pace your brain is hungry for. A few alterations a day can give your brain enough stimulating charge to brighten that lightbulb in your head.

"By changing your routines, you're moving away from relying on a set of well-worn mental paths," says Lawrence C. Katz, Ph.D. He suggests always looking for refreshing new opportunities to dampen the daily humdrum—rearranging your furniture, driving a new route to work, or wearing your watch on the opposite wrist. The visual change will shift your mind out of automatic mode and help forge new connections in the brain.

These changes may not help you remember 50 names instantly or prompt you to recall the text to the Gettysburg Address, but they do enhance overall brain fitness. "Varying routines allows you to have a larger repertoire of possible avenues for information to flow through your brain," says Dr. Katz. "You'll have a larger network to rely on for greater powers of association, greater creativity, and more flexibility in the way you think."

—Lawrence C. Katz, Ph.D., *is a professor of neurobiology at Duke University and coauthor of* Keep Your Brain Alive.

FOCUS YOUR ATTENTION THROUGH A 1-INCH FRAME

Lack of focus can interfere with memory. You can improve the power to focus by using a simple tool that keeps things in perspective.

In *Bird by Bird: Some Instructions on Writing and Life*, novelist Anne Lamott describes how the anxiety of starting a creative project can be so daunting that her brain either starts to spin or blacks out from overload. Her secret to getting the work done is rationalizing. "All I have to do is to write down as much as I can 'see' through a 1-inch (symbolic) picture frame. This is all I have to bite off for the time being."

"When your thoughts are scattered, setting boundaries can help you focus," says Susan Kavaler-Adler, Ph.D. If you are trying to recall the toast your best friend made at your wedding, think first about what you were wearing, then who was sitting at your table, then the sight of him standing with the glass in his hand, until finally he opens his mouth to speak the first line. This slowly expanding frame of reference will allow you to recall details by not being overwhelmed at "seeing" (and hearing) everything at once.

Pick up a 1-inch frame at the drugstore and keep it within reach at your work space. When you start to get overwhelmed by your work, sharpen your focus by looking through that symbol.

—Susan Kavaler-Adler, Ph.D., *a psychologist in Manhattan, is the founding director of the Object Relations Institute for Psychotherapy and Psychoanalysis, author of* The Compulsion to Create, *and leader of ongoing writing groups.*

TAP INTO THE MEMORY POWER OF SMELL

To preserve the vivid memory of an experience, link it to a scent.

Think of scent as a memory preservative. Having a specific odor that you repeatedly use in the same setting will help tap into your brain's powerful capability to make links and associations.

Smell is our most potent sense when it comes to memory. Certain neural pathways run straight from your nose to the hippocampus, the center of learning and memory in your brain.

"Unlike other senses, which have to go through a bunch of relay stations in the brain, smell has a direct line," says Lawrence C. Katz, Ph.D. "It's like the red telephone in the president's office that's directly linked to Moscow."

You can tag events in your life by tying them to a fragrance. For example, bake the same cinnamon buns when you're having the family over for Christmas every year. Peel an orange right before you dial a friend's phone number. Light a vanilla-scented candle whenever you do crossword puzzles.

By invigorating your odor universe and linking smells to experiences, you can send them straight to your long-term memory.

—Lawrence C. Katz, Ph.D., *is a professor of neurobiology at Duke University and coauthor of* Keep Your Brain Alive.

DINE OUT WITH YOUR FOREIGN TONGUE

If you thought learning a foreign language was tedious back in school, see if you prefer a classroom that has appetizers, ethnic music, and the aroma of baking bread.

Studying a new language provides the ongoing workout your mind needs to use it and not lose it. And by incorporating all of your senses into building your vocabulary, you'll be learning and bolstering your memory in five ways at once.

You'll learn faster and retain vocabulary better if you study while visiting the appropriate ethnic restaurant. Make a Spanish, Italian, or Chinese meal, for example, a class in itself.

When you visit the restaurant, bring your foreign language dictionary or vocabulary list to name common things like utensils and foods. Make a conscious effort to look at the colors of the walls, note the spices being used in the kitchen, and hear music or chatter. By involving all of your senses in the meal while taking in new vocabulary words, you've effectively increased the number of places where that memory exists within your brain, explains Joshua Landau, Ph.D.

"When you use all your senses, you're creating what's known as alternative representations—in other words, you're laying down additional memories that reinforce the memories you might want to draw upon later," says Dr. Landau.

But the foremost way to learn a foreign language is to speak it, so muster up your courage and order your meal in your new language. According to a University of Texas survey, people remember only 20 percent of what they hear, but 70 percent of what they say. Plus, scientists say that the burst of adrenaline you'll get from the stress of performing should solidify the new words in your memory.

—Joshua Landau, Ph.D., *is an assistant professor of behavioral sciences at York College of Pennsylvania.*

TURN UP THE LIGHT FOR BRIGHTER THOUGHTS

If your mind seems to get dull when it's dark, try using a light box to sharpen your thinking.

Have you ever found yourself looking out the window in despair at a cold, wintry day, thinking, "If only it were sunny, I'd be full of energy and ideas"? There's a good chance that you suffer from Seasonal Affective Disorder (SAD), a condition brought on by an adverse reaction to lack of light.

People with SAD may have difficulty thinking, says Maria Simonson, Ph.D. Other symptoms may include fatigue, sadness, headaches, and carbohydrate cravings. People with SAD also spend more time unemployed or on sick leave than other people, which means that they spend even less time stimulating their already-depressed brains.

Even if you don't have full-blown SAD (diagnosed by a doctor), you might feel blue during the winter months because of light deprivation. And your mood can affect your thinking.

Fortunately, your energy, memory, and creativity may return if you employ some of the phytotherapy (healing with light) treatments that have been developed for people suffering from SAD. In a study at the Institute of Clinical Neuroscience at St. Goran's Hospital in Stockholm, more than half of a group of 68 male and female volunteers with SAD improved markedly after a spending 2 hours a day in a room lit brightly enough to mimic sunlight.

You may get the same benefit by spending a half-hour every morning in front of a light box, says Dr. Simonson. Light boxes are specially designed devices that emit a much wider spectrum of light than normal lamps. They cost anywhere from $250 to $550 and can be purchased through healthy-living catalogs and online phytotherapy companies.

Using a light box in the morning seems to tackle the symptoms fastest, but it's best to check with your doctor before starting phytotherapy treatment, Dr. Simonson says.

—Maria Simonson, Ph.D., *is the director of the Health, Weight, and Stress Clinic of Johns Hopkins Medical Institutions in Baltimore.*

Mind Games

"The more active you keep your mind—through games or anything else that is mentally stimulating—the better your memory will end up being."

—Thomas H. Crook III, Ph.D.,
director of the Memory Assessment Clinic in Scottsdale, Arizona; president of Psychologix, a research organization in Scottsdale; and coauthor of The Memory Cure

DIAL M FOR MEMORY

Do you want to remember a phone number without looking it up? It may be as simple as thinking of your anniversary or your grandmother's birthday.

Merchants learned long ago that easy-to-remember phone numbers such as 1-800-VACUUMS are good for business. But they're not the only ones who can profit from this simple trick.

In fact, you can remember numerical sequences of any length by using catchy reminders, says Janet Fogler. If you want to remember a three-digit number, for instance, transform it into a time. So 235 becomes 2:35 P.M. Then, to further hardwire it into your memory, associate that number with what you're generally doing at that time of day, such as taking a coffee break or watching your favorite talk show.

Break a longer number down into smaller, more memorizable parts, Fogler suggests. So 402,111 becomes 40, 21, 11, which could be your age, the legal drinking age in your state, and your lucky number. You can also translate a number into a word using your telephone keypad. So 56,425,377, for instance, becomes "knickers."

—Janet Fogler *is a clinical social worker at Turner Geriatric Clinic at the University of Michigan in Ann Arbor and coauthor of* Improving Your Memory: How to Remember What You're Starting to Forget.

SAY A WORD
TO STAY WISE

A well-crafted acronym can help you recall even the most insignificant item on any shopping list.

Take the first letter from the name of each item you're trying to remember, then form those letters into a word, says Robert Finkel, Ph.D. If you need to buy hamburger, tuna, onions, ketchup, olive oil, cabbage, and radishes, you have the letters H, T, O, K, O, C, and R to work with. It doesn't seem too promising, does it? Rearrange them a little, and you just have to remember to buy HOTROCK while at the store.

The same can be done with errands you need to do (pay the PEC—power, electricity, and cable) or things you have to remember at work ("meet with FLEA"—Fred, Lisa, Erica, and Adam or "do FIRE"—filing, invoicing, reading, and e-mail).

If you don't have enough letters to make a full word, Dr. Finkel suggests you use a close-matching substitute. LIMPS, for example, is a good substitute for LMPZ because it will probably jog your memory as well, if not better, than a unrelated cluster of consonants.

—Robert Finkel, Ph.D., *is chairman of the department of physics at St. John's University in Jamaica, New York, and author of* The New Brainbooster.

STAKE OUT YOUR PEAKS

Whether a morning person or a night owl, everyone has an optimum time of the day for memorization.

If you are an early-to-bed, early-to-rise person, you're probably mentally sharp at quite different times than someone who stays up until the wee hours, says Douglas Herrmann, Ph.D.

Most people who work 9-to-5 jobs are at peak alertness sometime between 11:00 A.M. and 4:00 P.M. That peak time and its length can vary depending on your activity level, how much sleep you get nightly, and when and what you eat during the day.

Although each person's cycle of alertness is different, Dr. Herrmann says it's fairly easy to determine your own peaks. For several days, jot down when you feel sluggish and when you feel alert and clearheaded. You'll probably notice a pattern. Once you figure out when you're most alert, you can alter your schedule so that you can take advantage of your peak times.

"If you have creative or mental work you need to do, or memory tasks you have to perform, you'll have an easier time doing them when your energy reserves are at their highest," Dr. Herrmann says.

—Douglas Herrmann, Ph.D., *is the executive director of the Practical Memory Institute in Terre Haute, Indiana, and author of* Super Memory.

Form a Bond

You can make a lasting memory of a large list of items, simply by linking them together.

Break long lists down, then chain them all together, suggests Robert Finkel, Ph.D.

Let's say you want to remember the following words: sun, grass, potato, and pitchfork. Think of the bright, huge, glowing sun in the sky. Imagine its rays beating down onto the millions of tiny green blades of grass. Then visualize the grass quickly growing and spreading out, wrapping around a potato at the edge of a garden. Finally, imagine the potato taking out a sharp pitchfork to fend off the grass.

"The images can be absurd," Dr. Finkel says. "In fact, the more outlandish and imaginative they are, the better you'll remember them."

Aside from the absurd, you can form a link between the words if you use exaggerated sizes or numbers.

"Make sure you visualize each connection clearly before moving on to the next item," cautions Finkel. "Otherwise, your chain won't be strong enough to get you from that item to the the one after it."

—Robert Finkel, Ph.D., *is chairman of the department of physics at St. John's University in Jamaica, New York, and author of* The New Brainbooster.

LET GO

Turn a mental block over to the active powers of your subconscious and it can actually help you to remember.

The name of an actor or a popular song is on the tip of your tongue, but you can't quite think of it.

Instead of dwelling on the fact and driving yourself crazy, try forgetting all about it, recommends creativity consultant Roger von Oech. Instead, think of something entirely unrelated.

Think about high-school chums or a scene from your favorite movie. Focus on anything that will draw your mind away from that nagging void.

It will help keep your memory problem in perspective—you won't die if you can't recall the name of a song—so you'll relax a bit and probably think more clearly. And even though you consciously let go of your quest, you've planted a seed in the back of your mind. As you think about other things, something may cause that seed to blossom and the desired memory will pop into your head.

—Roger von Oech *is the president of Creative Think, a California-based consulting firm, and author of* A Kick in the Seat of the Pants.

SKETCH IN THE DETAILS

Instead of thinking in words or phrases, get creative and think in circles and arrows.

Imagine that you're learning about how the heart and lungs work. You could spend a lot of time writing down descriptions of what each organ does, or you could draw a quick sketch that takes the place of all of those words.

This is called telescopic thinking, says Robert Finkel, Ph.D. Start out with a basic figure like a circle that represents the heart. Then add a figure to represent the lungs and another to represent the body.

As you add to the picture, draw arrows from the heart to the lungs, where the blood gets oxygen and dumps carbon dioxide. Then draw arrows back to the heart and out into the body. As you learn more about the heart, you can break the circle down into parts representing the left and right atria and ventricles.

"You can do the same thing with maps, charts, and almost anything else," says Finkel. "It doesn't matter what shapes you choose or how you lay out the information, as long as you begin with the most simple bits of detail and then slowly add on to them, one step at a time."

—Robert Finkel, Ph.D., *is chairman of the department of physics at St. John's University in Jamaica, New York, and author of* The New Brainbooster.

QUIBBLE

Politicians and barstool philosophers do it every day. Why not you? Debate, the fine art of reasoned argument, can strengthen your logic and memory.

The next time you have an evening without any plans, find a friend who is willing to debate a controversial issue with you and invite him over, suggests Michael Chafetz, Ph.D. Pick the issue and then sit down and take a few minutes to jot down as many statements as possible either supporting or opposing the issue. Your friend should write down the other side of the argument.

When you're both finished, switch lists and take turns trying to find flaws in each other's arguments. "Learning to argue both sides of an issue is a great way to strengthen your logic and memory," Dr. Chafetz says. "By looking for gaps in logic, you'll help to exercise your mind and keep it sharp and focused."

If the argument is fun and lively, take it a step further. Wait a couple of days and invite the friend over again. This time, debate the issue from his perspective, but without using the list.

"This will force you to try to remember as many of your friend's points as possible, helping to improve your long-term memory," Dr. Chafetz says.

—Michael Chafetz, Ph.D., *is a neuropsychologist in New Orleans and author of* Smart for Life.

SPEAK SOFTLY TO MAKE MEMORY STICK

You might draw some stares, but verbalizing your thoughts and actions is a great way to remember them.

Research suggests that he who speaks, remembers. So talk to yourself to help focus your attention, eliminate distractions, and make things easier to recall, says Irene Colsky, Ed.D.

When you park at the airport, for example, talk to yourself as you get out of your car and walk into the terminal. Describe what you're doing, where you're at, what you're walking past, and what it looks like. Then, when you return from your trip and need to find your vehicle, turn your description around and walk through it in reverse. Odds are, you'll quickly hone in on your parking space.

"Making your mind consciously aware of where you're putting something or where you've left something will help you to recall that location later on," Dr. Colsky says.

Aside from remembering where certain objects are, this technique is also useful for remembering things like whether you've taken medication or vitamins or whether you've walked the dog or fed the cat—or any sort of mundane activity that might otherwise slip your mind.

—Irene Colsky, Ed.D., *is a professor in the department of teaching and learning in the School of Education at the University of Miami in Florida.*

GET REAL

A fact might not be very meaningful or memorable unless you can find a way to relate to it.

The human body contains 60,000 miles of blood vessels. Do you find that incomprehensible? Think of it this way: That's 10 round-trip drives from Los Angeles to New York. Chances are, you'll remember the second factoid more vividly.

"If a fact doesn't apply to you, you're going to have a much harder time remembering it," says communication expert Richard Saul Wurman. "So instead of taking a fact at face value, try to turn it into something you relate to."

If you're a sports fan, for example, find out how the size of an acre compares to the size of a football field or basketball court. To figure out the price of tea in China, learn about the Chinese exchange rate and how much of their money it takes to make a U.S. dollar.

"When you're learning something, ask questions that help you to clarify the information in a way that will help you understand it," says Wurman. "The bigger the connection turns out to be, the easier it'll be for you to recall a certain fact later on."

—Richard Saul Wurman *is a communications expert and author of* Information Anxiety.

UP THE ANTE

If your favorite board game suddenly seems monotonous, rise to the challenge and change the rules.

Jigsaw puzzles and games like chess or Scrabble really do stretch your mind, says Michael Chafetz, Ph.D. But after a while, almost any game or puzzle can become less engaging.

So whenever possible, add new rules. It will give your brain a real workout, Dr. Chafetz says. If you like chess, try playing blindfolded. Of course, you need a trustworthy opponent who will honestly describe each move. But as you picture the board in your mind, the game will stimulate your imagination, focus your concentration, and test your logic.

When you're playing Scrabble, require a minimum number of letters or insist that players use only certain letters. Increase the number of questions that need to be answered in Trivial Pursuit. Turn over jigsaw puzzle pieces so that you construct the blank side instead of the pictured one.

"Virtually any game can be brain-building if you think creatively and add challenges," says Dr. Chafetz. "Don't be afraid to tinker with the rules."

—Michael Chafetz, Ph.D., *is a neuropsychologist in New Orleans and author of* Smart for Life.

MAKE THE CONNECTION

If faces and names are a mishmash, try this process. It can help you turn any whoozit into a lasting memory.

After an introduction, use these simple techniques to solidify a person's name in your head.

First, make sure you hear the name, says memory expert Harry Lorayne. Most people are so busy with other things that they don't catch a person's name the first time it's said.

Second, spell out the name in your head immediately after hearing it. If you can't spell the name, ask the person to spell it for you. "You'll usually flatter the person by showing interest in his name," Lorayne says.

Third, comment on the name—if it's unusual, mention that. If you have a cousin with the same name, bring that up in your conversation. Anything that adds to the repetition and makes the name easier to remember will help, he says.

Fourth, use the person's name frequently during your initial conversation, Lorayne suggests. You should say it at least once or twice during regular conversation, and more often if you speak for a long time.

And fifth, when the conversation ends, say, "Nice meeting you, Mr. Jones," or "So long, Sally," instead of a generic goodbye. That adds to the repetition one more time and increases the odds that you'll remember the name in the future.

—Harry Lorayne *is a world-renowned memory expert and author of* Remembering People: The Key to Success.

PUNCH IN

Stick important tasks into a mental time clock, and you are apt to remember an entire list.

Make a list of at least six things you plan to do tomorrow. It can be anything from "going to work" to "going to lunch" to "mowing the lawn." Make sure that they are things that definitely will happen. Write each item down on an index card and file it under that day's date. Then, beside each item, estimate a time when the activity will take place, suggests Snowdon Parlette, Ph.D.

Leave the card at home and then, once at work, mentally begin to check off each item as it happens.

"Try to remember the exact time you wrote down for each activity," says Dr. Parlette. "It doesn't matter whether the estimation was correct—what's important is whether you remember the time you selected."

Write down each time you remember on a new card, and at the end of the day, compare what you remembered to what you wrote down the previous night.

"Each day, try to add one or two items to the list, and continue practicing for at least a couple of weeks," says Dr. Parlette. "It sounds like a simple exercise, but you'll be amazed at how your memory increases."

—Snowdon Parlette, Ph.D., *is a psychologist in New York City and author of* The Brain Workout Book.

REHEARSE KEY SCENES

Before opening night, actors have a dress rehearsal. Before any big event, you should rehearse, too.

If you're going to party where you'll be seeing a lot of people whose names aren't particularly familiar, the best thing you can do is spend some time beforehand imagining who you might meet at that gathering.

"Even if you know everybody who's going to be there, take a few minutes to review all their names and faces," Alan S. Brown, Ph.D., says. "If you're prepared in advance, you'll be more relaxed and more apt to remember other important details from the event."

After you arrive, if you see someone that you recognize but whose name temporarily escapes you, hone in on what you know about that person.

"Visualize where you first met the person and as many things as possible that you can remember about them," Dr. Brown suggests.

If you get nervous making introductions, practice prior to the actual event. "In the stress of the moment, people have forgotten the names of spouses and parents," says Dr. Brown. "Since you're more likely to blow an introduction while under stress, try practicing introductions with people you know, even if they already know each other. It'll help to build your confidence. If you have to introduce strangers, be sure to rehearse the names aloud to yourself beforehand for a little extra practice."

—**Alan S. Brown, Ph.D.,** *is a professor of psychology at Southern Methodist University in Dallas and author of* How to Increase Your Memory Power.

TUNE OUT

Distractions can make it more difficult to absorb and retain memories. But you can learn to overcome brain-busting chaos.

Read a book while a radio blares full-blast in the background. Or, if you prefer, watch different programs on two televisions simultaneously, suggests Francis Pirozzolo, M.D. These exercises can help you learn to filter out distractions and soak up new information even amidst pandemonium.

As you read, for instance, focus on the book and do your best to ignore the radio. Likewise, if you're watching two televisions, concentrate on one program and try to disregard the show on the other channel. (For a real challenge, make sure the volumes on both televisions are set at a similar level.) Stop after 10 minutes. See how much you can remember from the source you were reading or viewing.

Next, read the book, but this time also pay attention to the radio. Juggle your attention so that you don't lose track of what is occurring in the text or on the airwaves. Similarly, if you are watching two television programs, try to keep up with the action on both shows at once. Again, after 10 minutes, stop and see how much information you can recall from each source.

Do each of these exercises two or three times a week, and your ability to block out distractions should improve gradually.

—Francis Pirozzolo, M.D., *is a neuropsychologist at Baylor College of Medicine in Houston.*

RUMMAGE THROUGH THE ALPHABET

From A to Z, there are thousands of sleeping memories just waiting to be awakened.

How many times have you had an image or word crystal clear in your mind but still have been unable to say the right word out loud? According to Snowdon Parlette, Ph.D., you can help pry something from your mind by simply throwing some letters around in your brain.

Suppose you are trying to remember the name of a certain type of car. Start with the letter A: Acura, Accord, Aerostar? No. Then try B: Buick, Bonneville, Bronco? No. How about C: Camaro, Cadillac, Corolla. That's it, Corolla.

"By going through the alphabet in order, you're attacking the problem in an orderly and systematic way," Dr. Parlette says. "This gives you a much better chance of triggering at least a partial memory that may help you to remember the word, phrase, or object you're searching for."

Once you've latched onto the word or name in question, make up a rhyme or song that includes that object or person and set it to a familiar tune. It will help improve recall and prevent memory lapses in the future, he says.

—Snowdon Parlette, Ph.D., *is a psychologist in New York City and author of* The Brain Workout Book.

SPLICE TOGETHER A SOUND BITE

A silly sentence or phrase can help you remember a list of objects in a particular order.

Memorizing a list of seemingly unrelated words is easy, as long as you give the words a little order, says Michael Epstein, Ph.D., D.Ph. All you have to do is take the first letter of each word and form a sentence that you can remember. The result is called a mnemonic device.

For example, the order of the planets (Mercury, Venus, Earth, Mars, Jupiter, Saturn, Uranus, Neptune, Pluto) can be turned into the phrase "My very educated mother just served us nine pizzas," while the order of notes on the lines of the treble staff (E, G, B, D, F) becomes "Every good boy does fine."

In an everyday situation, you can concoct a phrase like "John ate my leg" to remind yourself to buy juice, apples, milk, and lettuce at the supermarket.

—Michael Epstein, Ph.D., D.Ph., *is a professor of psychology at Rider University in Lawrenceville, New Jersey.*

REWIRE YOUR VIEWING HABITS

Too much television erodes memory. But these steps can help you avoid couch potato brain.

Researchers at Kansas State University found that people's brain-wave activity began to diminish after just 15 minutes of television viewing—a direct indication that their minds were turning off.

No, you don't need to ditch the set, but instead of sitting there blankly, you can actually use the boob tube to boost your recall.

In fact, Thomas H. Crook III, Ph.D., says that television, used appropriately, can improve both your long-term memory and observation skills.

Whenever you watch television, take notes. Jot down quotes and note facial expressions, clothing, or unusual scenes, Dr. Crook says. Set the notes aside for a day or two. Then try to recall precisely what happened on the program without peeking at your notes. Once you've jotted down everything that you can remember, compare these recollections with the notes you took during the program. If you do this consistently, your accuracy should improve.

To really sharpen your mind, limit your television viewing. Make a list of the shows you want to watch each night. Turn the set on immediately before each program begins and turn it off immediately after it ends. That way, you won't be drawn into the next program or find yourself channel surfing for other shows, Dr. Crook says.

> **—Thomas H. Crook III, Ph.D.,** *is director of the Memory Assessment Clinic in Scottsdale, Arizona; president of Psychologix, a research organization in Scottsdale; and coauthor of* The Memory Cure.

MAKE THE PAST COME ALIVE

Use specific events such as weddings, births, graduations, or job changes as memory markers in your life.

If you can't pinpoint an exact date—say, the month or year when you moved into your first house—think about what else was going on in your life at that time.

"Things that happened to you long ago did not happen in isolation from other events," says Michael Pressley, Ph.D. "All you may need to remember a certain event is a marker or clue that will help you focus on your life at that instant."

Memories of popular songs, box-office hits at the movie theater, people you were dating, or even events of the time are all easy ways to help bring your memory back to a certain time frame.

"Once you have a certain memory from that period in mind, you'll begin to think of other details of your life, and that may be all you need to recall the memory you were looking for," says Dr. Pressley.

If not, your marker could at least provide you with a time frame that you can use for additional research either at the library or through friends or family members.

—-Michael Pressley, Ph.D., *is a professor of human development at the University of Maryland in College Park.*

TAKE SMALLER BITES

A list of 20 or 30 items will likely strain your memory beyond the breaking point. But you can remember it all, if you break that list down into mentally digestible chunks.

Long lists generally have a short shelf life in your noggin, says Francis Pirozzolo, M.D. So instead of biting off more than your brain can chew, compress titanic lists down into groups of five to nine items.

The process is called chunking, says Dr. Pirozzolo, and it works best when you break the list down into groups of common or related items.

Suppose you are preparing to write out holiday greeting cards. Scan through everybody you want to send a card, then compartmentalize people into easily remembered groups such as family members, coworkers, neighbors, college friends, and friends from your worship group.

The more closely related the items in each group are, the better your chances of remembering everything you need, he says.

Certainly, you can construct a written list to double

check at the end. But avoid consulting it until all of your cards are written out. Then compare the people you remembered with the ones on your list. If you've forgotten anyone, you can write out some more cards. But more than likely, you'll pat yourself on the back for recalling so many names without depending on a written inventory.

—Francis Pirozzolo, M.D., *is a neuropsychologist at Baylor College of Medicine in Houston.*

UNSCRAMBLE THE BRAMBLE

A jumble of random figures can improve your attention span and memory. So give your mind a mental workout with this brain-bending puzzle.

Ask a friend to make up a random block of numbers and letters like the one below. Any set of numbers and letters will do. Then, request that this person set a time limit and pick several numbers, letters, or combinations of both. Once you know what you're looking for, circle as many of the selected numbers and letters as you can within the given time. You might, for example, be asked to circle every 8 and S within 15 seconds.

```
N D 8 4 K L F 7 2 H S 8 4 J H S 7 S H S J S K S 9 S
D K 9 3 F O Z J H A S D D 8 7 3 H A H R A 9 3 H
Q 1 J F D 0 U F U 3 0 J L F D 0 U F U D S J D U F
S 0 9 4 3 J 0 U J D 9 3 J 0 3 D 0 K D 9 S K D D 8 0
S H D 8 2 O 2 0 D J S 0 A L D P F D 0 S D 8 3 K D
L D 9 M C N W 9 2 N 9 D N E 8 S H D K 9 8 J 3 S
```

To improve your memory skills, use a pencil to circle the chosen figures. After you finish, erase those marks. Then, several hours or days later, try doing the same grid again—this time looking for a different set of numbers or letters, says Vernon Mark, M.D. To improve your concentration skills, begin each exercise with a newly created chart of letters and numbers.

Dr. Mark recommends doing this exercise at least once or twice a week for maximum benefits.

—Vernon Mark, M.D., *is a Boston neurosurgeon and author of* Reversing Memory Loss.

SEND YOURSELF A SIGNAL

Traditional reminders have their places, but in a pinch, anything can do the job just as well.

There is some value in the old trick of tying a string around your finger in order to remember something. Of course, you may not always have a piece of string handy when you want to remember something, so reach for what you have at hand.

Memory expert Janet Fogler, for instance, uses her wedding band as a reminder.

"If I wake up in the middle of the night with a thought that I don't want to forget, I will turn my wedding ring around," Fogler says. "It stays that way until the morning and I will remember it without having to get up in the middle of the night to write it down."

If turning your wedding ring isn't practical, set alarm clocks around your home or office so that you don't forget to do important tasks at particular times. Send yourself an e-mail or leave yourself a reminder on your answering machine. Put something in an unusual but highly visible place—such as a slipper on top of a lamp—as a quirky reminder.

—Janet Fogler *is a clinical social worker at Turner Geriatric Clinic at the University of Michigan in Ann Arbor and coauthor of* Improving Your Memory: How to Remember What You're Starting to Forget.

DOWNLOAD LOTS OF BITS AND BYTES

Just like a computer, your brain has backup systems to help you find any given memory.

Memories tend to stick if you store them in more than one place in your brain. So create as many associations as you can—sights, sounds, smells—to help recall a particular idea or image, says Arnold B. Scheibel, M.D.

You can "attach handles" in several different places to each memory. The more handles you have, the easier it will be to grab one of them.

When you're looking for handles, go for vivid and imaginative associations. To make these associations, first repeat the information. If you're meeting a Mrs. Parker, for instance, help plant her name in your brain by saying it aloud: "Pleased to meet you, Mrs. Parker."

Second, make an emotional connection. Maybe Mrs. Parker reminds you of your favorite teacher, the one who used to play kickball with you during recess.

Finally, try to involve your senses. Pay attention to what you see, feel, smell, and hear when you're meeting Mrs. Parker, and you're more likely to remember her.

—Arnold B. Scheibel, M.D., *is a professor of neurobiology and psychology at the University of California at Los Angeles.*

EVERY PICTURE TELLS A STORY

Assign a mental image—even a silly one—to information, and you can tie it up in a neat bundle to be retrieved later.

Mental images often take up much less room in the brain than words or figures. That's why faces are often easier to remember than names. To take advantage of this trait in the brain, convert things you want to remember into pictures whenever possible, suggests Michael Epstein, Ph.D., D.Ph.

"If I met a man named John Woods," he says, "I'd immediately form a mental picture of a big lumberjack called Big John, walking through the forest, swinging an ax.

"I'd make the image active, because movement is much

easier to remember than, say, associating the name with a picture of an inactive tree."

In fact, the most important thing you can do is to ensure that your image is as vivid and lifelike as possible. And the more bizarre or off-kilter the images, the better.

"Instead of picturing a man chopping down a tree, I always picture the tree chopping the man down. Or, instead of having a horse eat an apple, have the apple eating the horse. Those are the kinds of things you remember," Dr. Epstein says.

—Michael Epstein, Ph.D., D.Ph., *is a professor of psychology at Rider University in Lawrenceville, New Jersey.*

WHEN ALL ELSE FAILS: ETCH IT IN FRUIT

Memory tricks and techniques are great, but when you absolutely, positively have to remember details, swallow your pride and grab a pencil.

If you really need to remember something and you don't trust your memory, write it down.

"Nobody can remember everything, especially if you're under an extreme amount of stress," says Barry Gordon, M.D., Ph.D. "That's why, for example, bank tellers write down the events of a robbery immediately after they occur. Then they have a record of their memories and they won't change when they talk to police or other people in the bank, whose questions might cause the memory of certain details to blur."

Carry a daily planner or a few index cards in your pocket or purse so you can write notes to yourself, Dr. Gordon suggests.

In addition, keep paper and a pen beside your phone, refrigerator, bed, and anywhere you else you spend a lot of time so that you have a place to quickly jot down reminders, he says.

If you find yourself ignoring paper reminders, look for unusual places to write reminders. If you have an important errand during your lunch hour, for instance, jot a note to yourself on a banana in your lunch bag. Or, if all else fails, take a black marker and make a note on your hand, where you won't be able to miss it.

—Barry Gordon, M.D., Ph.D., *is a behavioral neurologist at the Johns Hopkins School of Medicine in Baltimore and author of* Memory: Remembering and Forgetting in Everyday Life.

Mental
Nutrients

"Maintaining your memory is as simple as feeding your head."

—Julian Whitaker, M.D., *medical director of the Whitaker Wellness Institute in Newport Beach, California, and author of* The Memory Solution

IRON OUT MEMORY WRINKLES

You probably know that an iron deficiency can make you feel tired and sluggish. But it may put a wrinkle in your memory as well—especially for women.

Iron is crucial for chemical messengers in the brain, according to Ann B. Bruner, M.D. Studies show that people who are deficient in iron don't perform optimally on tests that involve memory.

While men usually store plenty of the mineral in their bodies, about 15 percent of women under age 50 are iron deficient or anemic because they lose iron during menstruation.

To maintain a healthy iron level, premenopausal women should aim for 15 milligrams daily; men and postmenopausal women need just 10 milligrams. Although most produce, grains, fish, and meat contain at least traces of iron, the best sources include 1 cup fortified cereal (varies from 4½ to 18 milligrams, depending on the brand), 3 ounces of beef liver (6 milligrams), 3 ounces lean sirloin (3 milligrams), ½ cup cooked spinach (3 milligrams), and ½ cup cooked beans (3 milligrams).

In addition, you can help your body get as much iron as possible from your food by avoiding iced or hot tea at mealtime (tea contains a compound that may block absorption). Instead, be sure to include a vitamin C-rich food or beverage such as strawberries, tomatoes, or orange juice with your meals, since vitamin C helps your body absorb as much iron as possible.

—Ann B. Bruner, M.D., *is assistant professor of pediatrics at Johns Hopkins University School of Medicine in Baltimore.*

SCUTTLE HIGH BLOOD PRESSURE

High blood pressure not only harms your heart, but attacks your brain as well. Fortunately, a healthy diet can help keep your blood pressure at an optimal level.

You can ward off changes in your brain cells that diminish your memory and ability to process information, if you keep your blood pressure under control. High blood pressure, especially if it begins in your forties or fifties, leads to the accelerated loss of brain cells, says Charles DeCarli, M.D.

In a study of 392 men, Dr. DeCarli found that those with the lowest blood pressures (on average, 114/74) performed best on memory and other cognitive tests. But you'll be helping to protect your brain as long as you can keep your blood pressure below 140/90, says Dr. DeCarli.

How can you accomplish that? A study of 459 men and women found that a low-fat diet rich in fruits, vegetables, and dairy products controlled high blood pressure just as effectively as medication, leading to an 11-point plunge in systolic pressure (the top number) and a 6-point dip in diastolic pressure (the bottom number).

Each day, the study participants consumed 7 or 8 servings of grains, 4 or 5 servings of vegetables, 4 or 5 servings of fruit, 2 or 3 servings of low-fat or fat-free dairy products, and 2 or fewer servings of meats, poultry, or fish. They also ate 4 or 5 servings of nuts, seeds, or legumes per week.

—Charles DeCarli, M.D., *is director of the Alzheimer's Disease Center at the University of Kansas in Kansas City.*

PLUG THE BRAIN DRAIN

Wouldn't it be great if you could slow down the brain's natural aging process and keep your memory as keen as ever? Maybe you can.

Research suggests that the nutrient acetyl-l-carnitine (ALC) protects cell membranes and increases energy production in aging brain cells. "It truly does extraordinary things for the brain," says Julian Whitaker, M.D.

In a study of people who have Alzheimer's disease, those who received ALC supplements for a year had a slower rate of deterioration in memory and intelligence than those who took placebos. Research in healthy people suggests that ALC supplements may improve attention span, memory, and coordination, says Dr. Whitaker.

He suggests taking 500 milligrams of ALC daily in two or three divided doses. If you don't notice an improvement in

2 to 3 weeks, increase the dose every other week until you reach 1,500 milligrams daily. Since long-term effects of this supplement are unknown, it's best to take ALC with a doctor's guidance. One more caveat: When shopping for supplements, don't confuse ALC with its close relative L-carnitine, whose role in brain health hasn't been established.

—Julian Whitaker, M.D., *is medical director of the Whitaker Wellness Institute in Newport Beach, California, and author of* The Memory Solution.

DON'T FORGET GINKGO

With all the new memory-boosting vitamin and mineral supplements, it's easy to overlook the old standby, ginkgo biloba.

In studies, this herb has a small-but-significant effect on the memories of people who have Alzheimer's disease. Researchers suspect that ginkgo may increase bloodflow by widening blood vessels or by inhibiting platelets. It also contains antioxidants, which prevent the formation of free radicals (unstable molecules that are harmful to the brain), says Barry Oken, M.D.

Unfortunately, scientists aren't sure how much the herb can help healthy people, but a large 7-year study is underway at the University of Pittsburgh. In the meantime, if you want to take gingko, Dr. Oken advises that you opt for 120 to 240 milligrams daily.

Be sure to read brand labels. You should choose a standardized extract of 24 percent flavoglycoside and 6 percent terpene lactones. One more warning: Don't use this herb without discussing it with a primary-care doctor who is knowledgeable about herbs, because ginkgo may interfere with some medications you're taking, especially blood thinners, MAO inhibitors, and nonsteroidal anti-inflammatory medications (NSAIDs).

—Barry Oken, M.D., *is an associate professor of neurology at Oregon Health Sciences University School of Medicine in Portland.*

REMEMBER THE AMINOS!

Your brain is almost completely regulated by amino acids. When your amino acids are in balance, you'll be able to think better.

Amino acids are the body's building blocks. Although most of us easily consume all of the amino acids necessary for good health, some are more important to memory than others. Of the 20 amino acids your body needs, here are the ones most crucial to brain function, along with suggestions for fitting them into your diet.

Tryptophan: It's the building block for the important brain messenger serotonin. Good sources: peanuts, oatmeal, bananas, beef, Swiss and Parmesan cheeses, turkey, string beans, tuna, and basil.

Phenylalanine: It helps make norepinephrine, a brain messenger involved in memory function. Good sources:

eggs, chicken, milk, chocolate, beef, brown rice, whole-wheat bread, shrimp, and tuna.

Tyrosine: It works with phenylalanine in the construction of brain messengers. Good sources: cheeses (all kinds) peanuts, oatmeal, bananas, milk, almonds, and sardines.

Arginine: It may bolster immunity; studies show that people who have Alzheimer's disease may have low levels of this amino acid. Good sources: poultry, peanuts, peanut butter, walnuts, and milk.

—**Arthur Winter, M.D.,** *is director of the New Jersey Neurological Institute in Livingston and coauthor of* Smart Food: Diet and Nutrition for Maximum Brain Power.

SPROUT ANTIOXIDANTS

When you're grocery shopping, it's tempting to linger at the bakery and rush by the radishes. But eating plenty of produce helps protect your memory far more than cream puffs ever could.

Fruits and vegetables are teeming with antioxidants, compounds that shield your brain cells from an attack by free radicals (unstable molecules that are harmful to the brain). Unchecked, free radicals interfere with the ability of your brain's chemical messengers to do their job, says James Joseph, Ph.D.

So how much produce do you have to pack into your diet for the antioxidants to outnumber the radicals? "Although Americans hear a lot about getting 5 servings of fruits and vegetables per day, our research suggests that closer to 10 servings would be optimal," says Dr. Joseph.

While eating a variety of fruits and vegetables ensures that you'll take in all of the different kinds of antioxidants, Dr. Joseph recommends that you include at least a few servings of the types of produce that contain the highest amounts of these brain boosters. Keep in mind that a serving can be as small as a medium-size apple or banana. Here are 10 fresh fruits and veggies that are richest in antioxidants (dried versions of these fruits pack a wallop as well).

- Alfalfa sprouts
- Blackberries
- Blueberries
- Broccoli florets
- Brussels sprouts
- Garlic
- Kale
- Plums
- Spinach
- Strawberries

—James Joseph, M.D., *is chief of the neuroscience lab at the USDA Human Nutrition Research Center on Aging at Tufts University in Boston.*

CLAMP DOWN ON CAFFEINE

A cup of java may jolt—or jeopardize— your memory, depending on when you start sipping.

Caffeine affects chemical messengers in your brain such as serotonin, which may help improve short-term memory, says Scott Terry, Ph.D. The catch: It seems to work only when you're feeling sluggish. If you're already aroused (maybe you're jittery about a big sales meeting) consuming caffeine may overstimulate you and hurt your memory. "Your best bet is to use caffeine only when you really need it to get going, like first thing in the morning," says Dr. Terry.

And remember, coffee is not the only source of caffeine. Most teas (herbals are the exception), coffee-flavored yogurt and ice cream, and certain carbonated sodas such as colas contain caffeine as well. So consider their possible impact on your memory before consuming them.

—Scott Terry, Ph.D., *is a professor of psychology at the University of North Carolina in Charlotte.*

TARGET B VITAMINS

Studies show that three members of the vitamin family—folic acid, B_6, and B_{12}— may ward off age-related memory loss.

When you don't get enough folic acid, your level of the amino acid homocysteine starts to climb, which may injure blood vessels in the brain. And a low folic acid, B_6, or B_{12} intake may narrow the carotid arteries, which are major transporters of blood to the brain, explains Katherine Tucker, Ph.D. In fact, a deficiency in B_{12} is fairly common in older people and is likely to be the cause of mental deterioration and confusion.

How can you ensure that your Bs are okay? Here are Dr. Tucker's recommendations.

• **Folic acid:** Aim for 400 micrograms daily (pregnant women may need more to prevent birth defects) but do not exceed 1,000 micrograms unless your doctor specifically advises you to take this much. Good sources: 1 serving fortified cereal (100 to 400 micrograms), 1 cup cooked pasta (100 micrograms), 1 cup dark green lettuce such as romaine (76 micrograms), ½ cup kidney beans (65 micrograms), 6 ounces orange juice (50 micrograms), ¾ cup cooked white rice (60 micrograms), and 2 slices sandwich bread (48 micrograms).

• **Vitamin B₆:** Shoot for 3 milligrams daily. "You can get that much from your diet, although you have to eat a lot of unprocessed foods like whole grains and produce," says Dr. Tucker. "People over 50 may want to consider taking a B₆ supplement of 3 milligrams just to be certain they're receiving enough." Good sources: banana (½ milligram), ½ avocado (½ milligram), 3 ounces roasted chicken (½ milligram), 3 ounces roasted pork (⅖ milligram), ½ cup cooked corn (¼ milligram), ½ cup cooked spinach (⅕ milligram) and ½ cup cooked brown rice (1/10 milligram). Be sure to avoid taking a dose higher than 100 milligrams without medical supervision since an excess of vitamin B₆ can cause serious problems like sensory neuropathy.

• **Vitamin B₁₂:** Strive for 8 to 10 micrograms daily from food and consider taking a multivitamin with at least 6 micrograms if you're age 30 to 50. Take a supplement with 25 micrograms if you're older than 50. "Although the Recommended Daily Allowance (RDA) of vitamin B₁₂ is just 2.4 micrograms, recent studies suggest that you may need much more of the nutrient to get the optimum level in your blood because in many people, it's very hard to absorb," says Dr. Tucker. Good sources: ½ cup clams (19 micrograms), 3 ounces baked salmon (5 micrograms), 3 ounces canned tuna (2 micrograms), 3 ounces lean beef (2 micrograms), 1 cup milk (1 microgram), and 1 cup low-fat plain yogurt (1 microgram).

—Katherine Tucker, Ph.D., *is an associate professor of nutrition epidemiology at the USDA Human Nutrition Research Center on Aging at Tufts University in Boston.*

SHAVE CALORIES

*You probably watch your calorie intake
only when you're trying to lose weight.
But you should keep a careful eye on it
for your brain as well as your brawn.*

Research from the University of Kentucky suggests that
eating no more than 1,800 to 2,200 calories per day—
300 to 1,000 calories less than the average American con-
sumes—will help your brain cells resist some of the
deterioration caused by aging.

Very low calorie diets, however, may hamper brain function. Mark Mattson, Ph.D., suggests that you discuss your appropriate calorie level with a dietitian. In general, women
should consume about 1,800 calories and men 2,000 to 2,200.

To trim excess calories from your diet, try the following:

- Switch from soda to water or diet beverages. Savings:
140 calories per 12-ounce serving
- Substitute fat-free milk for whole milk. Savings: 64
calories per cup
- Reach for a Peppermint Pattie rather than a Snickers.
Savings: 122 calories per bar
- Remove the skin from chicken breast. Savings: 27
calories per 3-ounce serving
- Have a dinner roll instead of a biscuit. Savings: 107
calories per piece

—Mark Mattson, Ph.D., *is chief of the laboratory of
neurosciences at the National Institute on Aging in Baltimore.*

MUNCH ON AN APPLE A DAY

*Eating an apple every day may help keep
the neurologist away. Apples are rich in
boron, an element that helps sustain
normal brain activity.*

Boron may help to keep your memory sharp, says James
Penland, Ph.D. His studies show that increasing boron intake from ¼ milligram to 3¼ milligrams daily improves performance on short-term memory tests up to 14 percent.
Fortunately, it's not hard to get this much boron in your diet.
Besides apples, particularly rich sources include broccoli,
grape and apple juice, peaches, cherries, carrots, potatoes,
cinnamon, and parsley. To satisfy your sweet tooth as well as
half of your daily boron needs, whip up this delicious dessert.

Warm Cinnamon Apples

        4 large baking apples such as Rome or Gala, cored
    ⅓–⅔ cup raisins
        4 teaspoons brown sugar
        2 teaspoons cinnamon
        3 tablespoons apple juice

Fill the apples with the raisins. Top with the brown
sugar and cinnamon. Pour the juice into a microwaveable
baking dish. Add the apples, cover with plastic wrap, and
cook on high for 6 to 8 minutes, or until soft. If using a
conventional oven, cover with foil and bake at 400°F for
30 to 35 minutes, or until soft.

Makes 4 servings

—James Penland, Ph.D., *is a research psychologist at
the USDA Grand Forks Human Nutrition Research Center in
North Dakota.* .

ZERO IN ON ZINC

Alphabetically, zinc always ends up at the bottom of the list of vitamins and minerals. But it's one of the front-runners for promoting brain health.

Zinc helps regulate communication between brain cells and is concentrated in the region of the brain that plays a large role in memory function. In addition, this trace mineral may calm nerve cells in the brain when they begin firing too rapidly, says Arthur Winter, M.D.

But you can get too much of a good thing. Large doses of zinc may cause nerve damage. So what's the best amount? Strive for about 15 milligrams daily, suggests Dr. Winter.

It's not hard to meet your zinc requirement, especially if you choose the following foods, which are terrific sources: 3 ounces lobster meat (7 milligrams), 3 ounces pork or lean beef (5 milligrams), ¼ cup wheat germ (3 milligrams), ½ cup crabmeat (3 milligrams), ½ cup cooked beans (3 milligrams), 3 ounces white-meat turkey (2 milligrams), ½ cup tofu (2 milligrams).

—Arthur Winter, M.D., *is director of the New Jersey Neurological Institute in Livingston and coauthor of* Smart Food: Diet and Nutrition for Maximum Brain Power.

DUNK YOUR BRAIN IN OLIVE OIL

Move over, margarine. So long, butter.
When it comes to memory, olive oil is the
unforgettable fat.

An Italian study found that participants who consumed the most olive oil and other monounsaturated fats, such as avocados and nuts, experienced less age-related memory loss than those who didn't eat as much of these healthy fats. The fatty acids in olive oil could help maintain the structure of neuron membranes, speculates Antonio Capurso, M.D. Olive oil's antioxidants may play a role as well.

Dr. Capurso recommends that you use olive oil instead of butter or margarine in all of your cooking. Here's one of his favorite recipes.

Country-Style Spaghetti

  4 tablespoons olive oil
  2 cloves garlic
  1 pound peeled tomatoes
3½ ounces pitted green olives
     Salt and pepper (optional)
12 ounces spaghetti

Heat the oil in a large sauté pan. Add the garlic and sauté until brown. Reduce the heat to low and gradually add the tomatoes. Cook for 10 minutes. Add the olives and salt and pepper, if using. Cook for 5 minutes. In the meantime, boil the spaghetti for about 5 minutes, or until it is nearly cooked. Drain and transfer to a large bowl. Add the sauce, mixing until well-coated.

Makes 4 servings

—Antonio Capurso, M.D., *works in the memory unit of the department of geriatrics at the University of Bari-Policlinico in Italy and is author of* Olive Oil: From Myth to Science.

STAY IN THE ZONE

When it comes to protein these days, people tend to eat too much or not enough.

Protein has been the focus of several popular diets. While getting plenty of protein is important for your brain (it may help ward off stress-related memory problems), you don't need the excessively high amounts suggested in these diets, says Asenath LaRue, Ph.D. In fact, high levels of protein could even lead to health problems such as kidney disorders and heart disease.

So what protein level will benefit your brain *and* the rest of your body? Women should shoot for about 50 grams daily while men require about 63 grams. Since many protein-rich foods are loaded with the type of fat that's terrible for your ticker, opt for these heart-friendly sources.

• Skinless chicken (21 grams per 3 ounces)
• Baked, broiled, or grilled fish (21 grams per 3 ounces)

- Lean beef (21 grams per 3 ounces)
- Low-fat plain yogurt (13 grams per cup)
- Fat-free or 1% milk (8 grams per cup)
- Cooked beans (7 grams per ½ cup)
- Tofu (7 grams per 3 ounces)

—Asenath LaRue, Ph.D., *is a research professor of psychiatry at University of New Mexico School of Medicine in Albuquerque.*

START THE DAY RIGHT

Mom was right all along. Breakfast very well may be the most important meal of the day.

When you skip breakfast, your work performance and thinking ability may suffer. In several studies, participants scored higher on memory-related tests after they had breakfast than when they took the exams without eating first.

With that established, scientists are now researching whether some breakfast foods boost your brain better than others. There are no definite results yet, says Robin Kanarek, Ph.D. In the meantime, she advises eating about 300 to 400 calories every morning—even if you're in a rush. And she doesn't mean doughnuts, muffins, and other sweets. Stash the following items in your desk drawer, briefcase, or glove compartment for the times when you have to leave the house on an empty stomach. Wash them down with a small carton of orange juice or fat-free milk.

- Cereal bars—which should have less sugar and fat than granola bars (130 to 150 calories each)
  - Dried fruit (80 calories per ¼ cup)
  - Peanuts (215 calories per ¼ cup)
  - Pretzels (110 calories per ounce)
  - Raisins (125 calories per ¼ cup)
  - Sunflower seeds (185 calories per ¼ cup)
  - Whole-grain crackers (20 calories each)

—**Robin Kanarek, Ph.D.,** *is a professor of psychology at Tufts University in Medford, Massachusetts.*

ACCENTUATE VITAMIN E

If you have trouble remembering where you put your keys or left your checkbook, you may have low levels of vitamin E in your blood.

Long linked to preventing heart disease, research suggests that vitamin E may play a role in memory as well. After analyzing the blood levels of vitamin E in nearly 5,000 people age 60 or older, scientists gave them two memory tests. About 11 percent of people with low levels of vitamin E experienced memory problems, compared to just 4 percent with high levels of the vitamin.

Scientists speculate that vitamin E may prevent memory loss by sweeping up free radicals, compounds that cause cell damage. But they're unsure about the optimum level of vitamin E you should consume, and whether getting the nutrient from food, supplements, or a combination of the two is best.

In the meantime, Siu Lui Hui, Ph.D., advises eating a diet rich in vitamin E and, if you want, taking a supplement of 400 international units (IU). Be sure to check with your doctor first because the nutrient may interfere with your medications or medical conditions.

Your doctor may recommend avoiding vitamin E supplements, for example, if you regularly take aspirin or a blood-thinning medication such as warfarin (Coumadin).

In addition, you can do the following to increase your intake of vitamin E:

- Sprinkle your cereal with wheat germ.
- Top regular or frozen yogurt with slivered almonds.
- Use salad dressings that are fortified with vitamin E.
- Spread peanut butter, instead of cream cheese, on your bagel.

—Siu Lui Hui, Ph.D., *is a professor of medicine at the Regenstrief Institute for Health Care at the Indiana University School of Medicine in Indianapolis.*

HOOK SOME SMART FOOD

You've probably heard speculations that fish is brain food. Scientists now know why it is marvelous for the mind.

The omega-3 fatty acids in fish help prevent clogged arteries, which can lead to strokes (something doctors now refer to as brain attacks). In addition, fish may also reduce inflammation and is rich in choline, a nutrient which is being studied for its involvement in the transmission of messages between nerve cells in the brain, explains Arthur Winter, M.D.

Dr. Winter suggests that you eat 3-ounce servings of fish—especially salmon, sardines, mackerel, lake trout, and herring—a few times per week. If you're not sure how to cook it, try this simple recipe for starters.

Salmon with Mango Salsa

4   salmon steaks, each about 1" thick
1   tablespoon olive oil
    Salt and pepper, to taste
½   cup jarred mango or other fruit salsa

Preheat the broiler. Wash the fish and pat dry. Brush one side of the fish with the oil and sprinkle both sides with salt and pepper. Broil the fish, oil side down, on a foil-lined baking pan 5 to 6 inches below the broiler for about 5 minutes. Turn the fish and broil for another 5 to 6 minutes until pink, but still moist. Remove from the broiler and top each piece with 2 tablespoons of salsa.

Makes 4 servings

—**Arthur Winter, M.D.,** *is director of the New Jersey Neurological Institute in Livingston and coauthor of* Smart Food: Diet and Nutrition for Maximum Brain Power.

HEAL WITH HUPERZINE

Scientists believe that this compound may be a powerful tool in treating memory problems, including some symptoms of Alzheimer's disease.

Huperzine A (Hup A), an extract from club moss, prevents an enzyme from destroying acetylcholine—one of the brain's most important chemical messengers that plays a fundamental role in cell-to-cell communication, says Alan D. Kozikowski, Ph.D. In Chinese studies of people who have Alzheimer's disease, four 50-microgram tablets of Huperzine A daily improved memory and brain function in 58 percent of the participants. Side effects such as nausea and dizziness were minimal. Other tests are underway, including a study at Johns Hopkins University in Baltimore.

Dr. Kozikowski recommends that older adults who have been diagnosed with Alzheimer's disease consider taking two 50-microgram tablets of Huperzine A in the morning and another two in the evening. Some Chinese studies also suggest that the extract can help older adults who suffer from less severe forms of memory loss. The supplement works similarly to donepezil (Aricept), a prescription drug used to treat Alzheimer's. Talk to your doctor before taking it to make sure that it doesn't interfere with your current treatment and to monitor any possible side effects.

—Alan P. Kozikowski, Ph.D., *is director of the Drug Discovery Program at Georgetown University Medical Center in Washington, D.C., and coauthor of* Huperzine A: What You Need to Know.

TRY THE NEW HERB ON THE BLOCK

For the past 20 years, Asians and Europeans have used the herbal supplement vinpocetine as a memory booster. But it only recently made its way to the United States.

Vinpocetine, an herbal extract derived from periwinkle seeds, seems to improve bloodflow, circulation, and oxygen use in the brain, according to Julian Whitaker, M.D.

"Research suggests that it's useful for both senile people and healthy young adults," says Dr. Whitaker. The recommended dose is 10 milligrams daily (usually the amount in 2 capsules). Side effects are rare, but may include low blood pressure, dry mouth, and weakness, so be sure to alert your doctor that you are taking vinpocetine.

> **—Julian Whitaker, M.D.,** *is medical director of the Whitaker Wellness Institute in Newport Beach, California, and author of* The Memory Solution.

MAGNIFY YOUR MEMORY

A shortage of magnesium can slow blood circulation in the brain and cloud your memory at crucial times.

Magnesium plays a role in regulating the stability of cell membranes and helps deliver nutrients to brain cells.

Running low on this mineral interferes with the transmission of muscle and nerve impulses, which delays the processing of memories, says Thomas H. Crook III, Ph.D.

Women require 310 to 320 milligrams of magnesium daily; men need 400 to 420 milligrams. It's not difficult to meet those requirements with a healthy diet, says Dr. Crook. Just incorporate some of these magnesium-rich foods into your eating plan: 1 cup cooked spinach (155 milligrams), ¼ cup almonds (105 milligrams), 3 ounces baked halibut (90 milligrams), 1 cup cooked brown rice (85 milligrams), 1 cup cooked beans (80 milligrams), and 2 slices whole-wheat bread (50 milligrams).

—Thomas H. Crook III, Ph.D., *is director of the Memory Assessment Clinic in Scottsdale, Arizona; president of Psychologix, a research organization in Scottsdale; and coauthor of* The Memory Cure.

BREW BRAIN POWER

Gotu kola sounds more like a zippy soft drink name than a memory-boosting herb. But it has been nicknamed "food for the brain," with good reason.

Gotu kola, a plant with fan-shaped leaves that grows in India, South Africa, and the tropics, helps improve concentration and memory by enhancing the activity of an important chemical messenger in the brain, says Mark Stengler, N.D. Despite the strikingly similar name, it's not related to the kola nut and it doesn't contain caffeine.

Dr. Stengler recommends taking 120 milligrams of gotu

kola daily in a standardized extract unless you are pregnant or breastfeeding. You can also use dried gotu kola leaves in a tea. For the ultimate in memory-boosting and relaxation, try one of Dr. Stengler's favorite brews, which stars gotu kola. Steep ½ teaspoon dried gotu kola, ½ teaspoon dried nettle, ½ teaspoon dried peppermint, and ¼ teaspoon dried lemon balm in 2 cups of boiled water for 10 minutes.

—Mark Stengler, N.D., *is a naturopathic doctor specializing in herbal medicine in San Diego and author of* The Natural Physician.

NAIL CHOLESTEROL BEFORE IT HAMMERS YOU

If you manage your cholesterol, you'll decrease your risk of stroke and keep your pipeline to the brain flowing freely.

High cholesterol can thicken the carotid artery, the large vessel in your neck that sends blood to your brain, says Lynn Smaha, M.D. According to the American Heart Association, you should aim for a total cholesterol level of less than 200 milligrams per deciliter (milligrams/dl). If a cholesterol test shows your level is high, and especially if you have a lot of LDL, or "bad" cholesterol (higher than 130 milligrams/dl), take these steps immediately to begin lowering it.

• **Shrink the saturated fat in your diet.** Remove the skin from chicken, switch to low-fat dairy products, and go easy on butter and red meat. Products with the American Heart Association check on the label are low in saturated fat.

- **Cut back on cholesterol-rich foods.** Limit your diet to no more than 300 milligrams of cholesterol—200 milligrams if you already have heart disease. High-cholesterol foods include egg yolks and red meat.
- **Get off the couch.** Exercise—walk, bike, garden—for 30 to 45 minutes at least three times a week.
- **Go for whole grains.** Oatmeal, whole-wheat bread, brown rice, and other whole grains pack a lot of fiber, which helps reduce cholesterol.

—Lynn Smaha, M.D., *is president of the American Heart Association and practices cardiology at the Guthrie Clinic in Sayre, Pennsylvania.*

TRY THE MEMORY HORMONE

A supplement of DHEA, an adrenal hormone, may help you feel more alert and jumpstart your memory.

DHEA (short for dehydroepiandrosterone) is produced by the adrenal glands and synthesized in the skin and the brain. Your levels of the hormone drop as you age, says Julian Whitaker, M.D. And people with Alzheimer's disease may have particularly low levels—about half as much as healthy people of the same age. "We're not sure how DHEA affects your brain, but we think it might combat chronic stress, which damages the part of the brain that processes memory," says Dr. Whitaker.

He suggests that people over 45 take a DHEA supplement marked "pharmaceutical grade" to ensure purity. Men should opt for 50 to 100 milligrams of DHEA. Women should take 25 to 50 milligrams.

Avoid the hormone if you have prostate cancer. Although there's no link between the two, your body converts DHEA to testosterone, which may fuel the growth of tumors. The supplement is also not recommended for men and women under age 35 since it could suppress the body's natural production of DHEA. Take DHEA under medical supervision so that your doctor can monitor possible side effects such as irregular heart rhythms and liver damage.

—Julian Whitaker, M.D., *is medical director of the Whitaker Wellness Institute in Newport Beach, California, and author of* The Memory Solution.

SNAG A SNACK

For years, munching between meals had a bad reputation for causing everything from weight gain to cavities. But if you choose smart snacks, your brain and body will benefit.

A midafternoon snack of 200 to 250 calories improves your performance and memory. "A snack seems to offset the sluggish feeling and dip in performance that many people experience a few hours after lunch," says Robin Kanarek, Ph.D.

Although any snack would probably do the trick, Dr. Kanarek recommends including at least one serving of a fruit or vegetable as part of your choice because produce is loaded with nutrients that will keep you healthy.

Next time you're experiencing the 3:00 P.M. brain drain, reach for one of these nutritious munchies.

- Banana topped with 1 tablespoon peanut butter
- 5 whole-grain crackers, 1 ounce part-skim mozzarella cheese, and ½ cup seedless grapes
- 6 ounces orange juice and English muffin topped with 1 tablespoon jelly
- 4 small vanilla wafer cookies, 6 medium strawberries, and 8 ounces fat-free milk
- 1 cup plain low-fat yogurt mixed with ⅓ cup blueberries and 1 tablespoon chopped walnuts

—Robin Kanarek, Ph.D., *is a professor of psychology at Tufts University in Medford, Massachusetts.*

PS: YOUR BRAIN WILL LOVE THIS

A nutritional supplement made of soy seems to be able to rejuvenate the membranes of your brain cells.

The supplement phosphatidylserine (usually abbreviated to PS) stimulates the production and release of chemical messengers that pass information from one cell to the next, explains Thomas H. Crook III, Ph.D. In a study of 500 patients, Dr. Crook found that people who took PS for 12 weeks showed a 33 percent increase in the ability to re-member names 1 hour after introduction compared to just a 9 percent improvement among those taking the placebo.

If you're age 40 or over, Dr. Crook recommends taking 300 milligrams of PS daily for a month and then cutting back to 100 milligrams per day. "While PS occurs naturally in foods such as fish, soy products, and green leafy vegetables, our needs increase as we age and, at that point, we can get enough only through a supplement," says Dr. Crook. One caveat: Some manufacturers sell PS as part of a "PS complex" which includes substances other than this active ingredient. In general, these complexes contain only meager amounts of actual PS, so taking it solo is a better way to ensure an adequate dosage.

—Thomas H. Crook III, Ph.D., *is director of the Memory Assessment Clinic in Scottsdale, Arizona; president of Psychologix, a research organization in Scottsdale; and coauthor of* The Memory Cure.

Smart Moves

"Your brain is the most important piece of real estate that you own. You need to keep mentally and physically active to maintain its value."

—Paul Spiers, Ph.D., *clinical neuropsychologist, Massachusetts Institute of Technology in Cambridge*

TAKE A "NOVEL" APPROACH

Reading is a time-tested brain booster
that helps keep your memory strong.

Reading is one of the best ways to improve all of your brain's many functions. "It increases the number of active cells in your brain," says Charles A. Weaver III, Ph.D., "and the more active cells you have, the more connections you have between neurons, the active cells of the nervous system." When you read, you make use of parts of the brain that you don't rely on for other activities. You have to connect words to sentences to paragraphs and then put it all in context.

Any kind of reading is helpful, according to Dr. Weaver. Even light reading can exercise your mind and improve your memory skills. So skim the morning's headlines in your favorite newspaper. At night, peruse a few chapters of a good novel, a biography, or even a joke book, Dr. Weaver suggests.

Want to retain more of what you read? Take a break every 20 or 30 minutes to ask yourself questions about what you've just read. The more you reflect on the material, the more likely it will stick with you, Dr. Weaver says.

—Charles A. Weaver III, Ph.D., *is an associate professor of psychology and neuroscience at Baylor University in Waco, Texas.*

FEED YOUR BRAIN
THE WRITE STUFF

Writing helps to clarify your thoughts
and improve your memory.

Writing, like reading, is a complex mental task. You have to think about what you want to say, choose the right words to convey your message, and connect words to make sentences and then paragraphs. Depending on the material, you may be exercising your creativity too.

Even if you don't fancy yourself a wordsmith, try to write at least one letter a week, suggests Alan S. Brown, Ph.D. You might use that opportunity to share memories, renew a friendship, get in touch with family members, or even create a kind of newsletter that goes out to a number of people. If you have a bone to pick with a recent editorial in the newspaper, write a rebuttal to the article.

If you have a computer and access to the information highway, there are hundreds of e-mails just waiting to be written. Many people report that e-mails revitalize relationships with friends they haven't corresponded with in years. Every time you write one, you're giving your mind a boost.

—Alan S. Brown, Ph.D., *is a professor of psychology at Southern Methodist University in Dallas and author of* How to Increase your Memory Power.

SIDETRACK SIDE EFFECTS

Numerous prescription and over-the-counter drugs can dampen memory and trigger confusion.

Many medications affect your mental abilities. Here are some to watch out for, according to W. Steven Pray, Ph.D., R.Ph.

- Over-the-counter sleeping pills or antihistamines, such as Benadryl and Tylenol PM, that contain diphenhydramine.
- Any medication containing alcohol, which can cause confusion and temporary memory loss.
- Over-the-counter sinus products, such as Sine-Off and Sinutab, that contain memory-inhibiting antihistamines.
- Prescription tranquilizers such as triazolam (Halcion). "Some people used to take Halcion to combat jet lag and they wouldn't remember anything about the entire trip. It caused a horrible memory loss," Dr. Pray says.
- Antianxiety medications such as benzodiazepines (Xanax); antidepressants such as amitriptyline (Elavil); pain medications such as narcotic analgesics (Darvocet or Percocet); and high blood pressure medications like methyldopa (Aldomet) or propranolol (Inderal).

Drug interactions also can disturb memory. So if you are taking any medication and develop memory problems, consult your doctor or pharmacist, Dr. Pray suggests.

—W. Steven Pray, Ph.D., R.Ph., *is a professor of nonprescription drug products at Southwestern Oklahoma State University in Weatherford.*

CLEAR THE DECKS

*With less clutter and better organization,
you can devote more brain power to
what is really important.*

Assign a fixed location to items such as medications, important phone numbers, valuable papers, tools, keys, and your wallet, suggests Jordan Grafman, Ph.D. If you know where things are and can find them easily, you cut down on frustrating searches that tax your brainpower.

Every time you put an item in a random spot, he explains, your brain has to find a place to store that random bit of information. But if you have a routine, it reduces the burden. "The idea is to get rid of clutter in your mind, so you can remember the things that are really important," says Dr. Grafman.

Here are some tips that will help you organize some details in your life so that you can remember more.

• If you take a number of medications, list them all and always keep them in the same place. If you have medications you take around mealtime, store them in the kitchen. Medications taken before bedtime should be next to your toothbrush. Or use a pill organizer with separate, sequential compartments for medications that you take throughout the day.

• Have a small basket near the front door. Put your keys in the basket whenever you walk in the door. You'll never have to waste brainpower searching for your keys again.

• Make two lists of important phone numbers—one to tape in a prominent place in the house, the other to carry in your wallet or purse.

—Jordan Grafman, Ph.D., *is chief of the cognitive neuroscience section at the National Institute of Neurological Disorders and Stroke.*

UNCORK TENSION

When stress takes over, your brain is affected. To remember things better and concentrate more easily, take steps to reduce stress.

Some evidence suggests that high levels of stress may actually shrink the part of the brain that governs learning and memory. "You may find that you forget all kinds of things," says Alan S. Brown, Ph.D., "even where you're going and what you're doing."

But if you can learn to cope with stress in constructive ways, you might regain much of your mental nimbleness.

Start with meditation, yoga, and other traditional relaxation techniques. In addition, here are some creative ways to help reduce stress.

- Burst some bubbles. Popping bubble wrap (sealed air capsules used in packaging) can help reduce stress, according to researchers at Western New England College in Springfield, Massachusetts.
- Create a quiet haven. One quiet room—or even a corner of a room—can become a private oasis where you can retreat to sip tea, listen to music, and forget about the day's tensions.
- Keep a "worry" log. Write down whatever is making you tense. "Just being aware of the stresses in your life helps free up memory space," says Dr. Brown.

—Alan S. Brown, Ph.D., *is a professor of psychology at Southern Methodist University in Dallas and author of* How to Increase your Memory Power.

JOG YOUR MEMORY

People who exercise have better memories than those who don't. If you can get into a routine of regular exercise, expect to improve your alertness and brainpower.

Regular exercise appears to boost the production and functioning of neurotransmitters, the chemical messengers that ferry information from one portion of the brain to another. Animal studies also suggest that aerobic exercise stimulates the growth of blood vessels and improves blood-flow in the brain.

Even sedentary people who start exercising for the first time can improve their mental abilities, and consequently their memory, by 20 to 30 percent, says Barry Gordon, M.D., Ph.D.

It doesn't take a whole lot of exercise to hone your memory skills. Do at least 20 to 30 minutes of moderate aerobic activity such as walking, swimming, running, or biking at least three or four times a week and you'll certainly notice a difference.

Even minor changes in your daily exercise habits can have an impact, such as walking up stairs instead of taking an elevator or escalator. In fact, wherever you go, try to do as much walking as you can. Every step brings you that much closer to mental agility.

—Barry Gordon, M.D., Ph.D., *is a behavioral neurologist at the Johns Hopkins School of Medicine in Baltimore and author of* Memory: Remembering and Forgetting in Everyday Life.

SWING YOUR PARTNER

Do some dancing to stimulate your brain and tweak your memory.

Dance is a great way to move your body, challenge your mind, and improve your memory all at the same time, says Sherry Willis, Ph.D. She recommends it because of the aerobic exercise combined with the requirements of remembering dance steps.

Square or contra (English country style) dancing may be especially good. You get a chance to kick up your heels and exercise your mind at the same time, Dr. Willis says. These dances require intense concentration and spatial awareness. Plus, you have to listen to the caller, follow his directions, work with a partner, and then do the steps.

"You have to master a series of remembered moves in order to succeed," Dr. Willis says. "It requires a fair amount of mental gymnastics."

Many square and contra dances have an orientation session for beginners before the official dance starts. During the session, the caller will teach the group each separate square or contra dance, so it's possible for even inexperienced dancers to get into the swing. The good news for singles is that you don't have to bring a partner. In fact, you'll probably dance with half the room before the dance is over.

—Sherry L. Willis, Ph.D., *is a professor of human development at Pennsylvania State University in State College. She devises strategies to help older people maintain cognitive skills as they age.*

HIT THE BOOKS

*Acquiring any kinds of new skills—
from algebra and archery to French
and fencing—can help give your brain
a boost.*

Adult education provides an excellent mental workout, says Richard Mohs, Ph.D. The more unfamiliar the subject matter, the better because new activities stimulate the brain and generate lasting memories.

Education turns on the biochemical machine that makes new proteins in the brain, Dr. Mohs says. These new proteins strengthen connections between brain cells, and in turn, can offset many of the degenerative changes and memory lapses associated with age.

Most community colleges and adult evening schools offer a range of interesting classes. But you don't even have to go to traditional classes. You might ask a friend who has a skill you admire—whether she's a gifted artist or a talented chef—to give you informal lessons. Or make regular trips to your local library for information about lectures, art exhibits, or discussion groups. As long as you expose yourself to new ideas that interest you, you'll be motivated to learn and your brain will benefit from the experience.

—Richard Mohs, Ph.D., *is a professor of psychiatry at the Mount Sinai School of Medicine of New York University in New York City.*

INHALE MEMORIES, EXHALE WORRIES

Anxiety dampens your ability to recall faces, places, names, and other vital information. But a simple breathing technique can settle your racing mind and boost your recall.

Public speakers, actors, and other artists all do one thing before they perform: They take a few deep breaths to help ease nervousness.

"Memory works best when the mind is relaxed," says memory researcher Danielle Lapp. She advocates deep breathing to help you achieve that relaxation. Here's how.

- Sit comfortably, letting your arms and legs go limp.
- Imagine yourself on a beach, watching waves gently rolling into shore. Visualize a steady flow of waves, trying to hear the water movement, and even smell some salty air.
- Keeping your mouth closed, inhale through your nose deeply and gradually until your lungs and stomach feel full.
- Exhale slowly, again through your nose, until all of the air is expelled.
- Continue breathing deeply, listening to the rhythm of your breathing.

As you pay attention to inhalation and exhalation, tune into your image of waves. Inhale as a wave builds, and when your lungs are completely full, picture the wave at its crest. Slowly exhale, taking a long, smooth ride on the wave in to shore. Try to make the exhalation last twice as long as the inhalation. Do this until you feel your anxiety float away.

—Danielle Lapp *is a memory-training researcher at Stanford University and author of* Don't Forget! Easy Exercises for a Better Memory.

SHIFT GEARS

If you're wading through reams of paper or glued to a computer monitor, be sure to take some time for breaks.

It's virtually impossible to learn or recall something if you can't concentrate. So whenever you're working on a project, take a 5-minute break every 30 minutes or so. Odds are, you'll remember more than if you tried to gulp all that information down in one marathon session, says Arnold B. Scheibel, M.D.

"Your brain can only absorb information for as long as you can endure sitting," Dr. Scheibel says. "I call it the brain-buttocks rule."

During each break, get up, walk around for a few minutes, and then do a couple of stretching exercises. To stretch your shoulders and upper back, for instance, hold a towel in your right hand. Raise and bend your right arm over your right shoulder so that the towel dangles down your back. Grasp the bottom end of the towel with your left hand. Gradually, grasp higher and higher up the towel with your left hand, as high as you can. As you do this, you'll find that it also pulls your right arm down. Continue until your hands touch, or as close to that as you can comfortably go. Switch hand positions and repeat on the left side.

—Arnold B. Scheibel, M.D., *is a professor of neurobiology and psychology at the University of California at Los Angeles.*

STORE WHILE YOU SNORE

A good night's rest is an essential activity break for your brain—and you need that break to maintain a strong memory.

The process of storing memories goes clipping along while your brain is in its deepest dream state, known as Rapid Eye Movement (REM) sleep. While your eyes are moving rapidly beneath your securely shut lids, your brain is doing a remarkable amount of necessary processing. If this is disrupted for any reason, the information your brain was storing at that moment will be permanently and irreversibly damaged, says Charles A. Weaver III, Ph.D.

"Storing memories is like freezing ice cubes in a tray," Dr. Weaver explains, and sleep is essential to the solidification process.

To get some of that REM sleep every night, most of us require 6 to 8 hours of rest. Here are some ways to ensure that you get the good night's sleep that you need for maximum memory storage.

- Exercise in the morning or early afternoon—not just before you go to bed. If you work your muscles just before you hit the hay, the increase in your heart rate, respiration, and other nervous system activities might interfere with your sleep.

- Avoid caffeinated drinks, such as coffee, tea, or soda, within 2 hours of bedtime. In fact, your caffeine curfew might have to be even earlier. Some people are affected if they drink caffeine even 4 hours before lights-out.

- Keep your bedroom dark and quiet.

- Set your bedroom temperature at a moderate 60 to 65°F.

- To maintain a healthy sleep routine, try to go to bed and get up at the same time every morning, even on weekends.

- Don't forget sex. For some people, it's the perfect intro to restful sleep.

—**Charles A. Weaver III, Ph.D.,** *is associate professor of psychology and neuroscience at Baylor University in Waco, Texas.*

QUESTION AUTHORITY

Don't be afraid to let your ignorance show. If you don't know much about something, keep asking until you understand. The new information is more likely to stick in your brain if you really understand it.

One way to avoid information overload is to make the speaker slow down—and to hear more about one particular topic, says Dennis Gersten, M.D. The next time someone mentions an unfamiliar book, author, politician, or event, stop the conversation and start asking questions. Otherwise, the other person is likely to skip to the next topic before you've even started to digest the first topic.

If you're not afraid to ask questions, people will probably respect you for being courageous and curious, Dr. Gersten says. Ultimately, you'll understand and remember better because you get a longer look at the whole picture.

> **—Dennis Gersten, M.D.,** *is a psychiatrist in private practice in San Diego and author of* Are You Getting Enlightened or Losing Your Mind?

SEE THINGS EYE-TO-EYE

Visual contact is one of the best ways to focus your attention and retain vital information.

It happens all the time at weddings, high-school reunions, and other social gatherings. You're talking with a casual acquaintance when, out of the blue, you spot a longtime friend on the far side of the room. Odds are, from that point on, you don't remember what was said by the person who's speaking to you. You're too busy thinking about the other person on the far side of the room.

There's a simple reason for it. When your gaze wanders, so does your attention, says Tora Brawley, Ph.D. In any situation, you're more likely to recall what someone says if you maintain eye contact with them. So in order to better remember what someone is saying, be sure to keep looking at the person who is chatting with you. And if you do get momentarily distracted, refocus your attention on the speaker's eyes as soon as possible. It will help you quickly get back into the flow of the conversation.

Once you refocus, don't be shy about asking your companion to repeat the information you missed. In the long run, it's much more polite than playing dumb about a detail, which may keep you in the dark for the rest of the conversation. And when you're less engaged, your mind is more likely to wander again.

—Tora Brawley, Ph.D., *is a clinical neuropsychologist at the University of South Carolina School of Medicine in Columbia.*

SEND IN THE CLOWNS

Do you seriously need to remember something? Then take time to laugh.

Mirth increases bloodflow to the brain, arouses the senses, promotes creativity, and increases the likelihood that you'll absorb new information, says William F. Fry, M.D. If you need to memorize a speech, for instance, take a break from your work every 20 to 30 minutes and allow yourself to engage in some frivolous activity. Flip through a joke book, read the daily comics, or just make a funny face in the bathroom mirror. You'll feel refreshed, more enthusiastic, and in a better frame of mind to imagine a dynamic interaction with the audience that's going to hear your speech.

Better yet, find ways to make others laugh. Post a cartoon where others can enjoy it. Call or e-mail a good one-liner to a friend. The creativity involved in those moments will jump-start your brain and rewire it a bit so that new information is easier to grasp.

Laughter is also one of the best antidotes for memory problems associated with depression, Dr. Fry says. A stockpile of cartoons, funny newspaper stories, and humorous videos can do wonders for you when you're feeling blue. As your mood improves, so will your powers of recall.

—William F. Fry, M.D., *is a psychiatrist and professor emeritus at Stanford University School of Medicine.*

FEELING LOW? GET BACK TO BASICS

Depression makes it harder to retain new information and recall memories. So if you're feeling blue, don't overload your brain.

When we feel down in the dumps, we tend to brood—and that's no time to put your memory to the test, says Tora Brawley, Ph.D. "When you're really feeling low, there can be changes in your brain chemistry that can affect your memory and concentration," she says.

Even if you normally have a good memory, give yourself a break when you're in a gloomy frame of mind. Go ahead and make more lists than you normally would, Dr. Brawley suggests. Write reminders to yourself about bills that need to be paid and errands that need to be run. When you start to feel better, you'll probably find your powers of concentration bounce back, and those lists and reminders might not be necessary.

Since you're in list mode, some other important items to jot down are goals you want to accomplish in the next week or month. Think of activities that make you feel vibrant and that will offer a deep sense of accomplishment, like planting flower bulbs or hosting a dinner party. Staying social and active gives you a sense of purpose for the future and can get you out of your rut much more quickly than brooding or isolating yourself.

Of course, if you feel severely depressed for more than 2 weeks or have *any* suicidal thoughts, you should talk to a doctor immediately.

—Tora Brawley, Ph.D., *is a clinical neuropsychologist at the University of South Carolina School of Medicine in Columbia.*

Alternative Options

Studies clearly show that alternative medicine has solutions to increase flagging memory, concentration, and learning ability.

Expect holistic healers to investigate both psychological and physical issues to determine the root of your memory problems. If, for example, anxiety, sleeplessness, or poor self-esteem are causing your memory problems, alternative practitioners have a wide array of healing techniques to improve your mental health. You may be given herbs or guided meditation techniques to relax you, or you may be taught hypnosis to build your confidence.

In the end, a holistic healer's prescription for your good health will likely be more personalized than that of a conventional medical doctor, and more natural. Expect practitioners to help you make overall lifestyle changes that will provide other health benefits in addition to enhanced memory.

Another asset of natural remedies is that they have fewer side effects than traditional Western treatments. But as with any medical treatment, you would be wise to use alternative healing techniques as part of a comprehensive program recommended by a well-trained practitioner. Use the following guide as a resource to select a healer who has the background to aggressively stem your memory loss.

Ayurvedic Medical Specialists

Practitioners of Ayurvedic medicine, a 5,000-year-old healing system originating in India, consider memory loss to be an imbalance of the *vata* form of energy—one of the three principal energies or facets of one's being.

The goal of Ayurvedic medicine is to help correct any imbalance in the body's three principle energies. To improve vata energy, the practitioner is likely to prescribe a diet filled with sweet, salty, and sour foods. You may also get a number of Ayurvedic herbs that improve concentration, such as ashwagandha or brahmi, says Scott Gerson, M.D., director of the National Institute for Ayurvedic Medicine in Brewster, New York. The herbal doses may be in the form of teas or powders.

One truly pleasurable treatment is the Ayurvedic practice of dripping hot oil on the forehead, thought to penetrate the brain and improve blood circulation. For enhancing mental capacities, some Ayurvedic doctors use enemas to cleanse the body and promote good health. They also recommend gentle exercise, such as yoga postures or a walking program.

For help in locating an Ayurvedic doctor, write to the National Institute of Ayurvedic Medicine at 584 Milltown Road, Brewster, NY 10509.

Herbalists

Before Anacin, Tylenol, and Dramamine came along, people relied on herbs. In fact, herbal home remedies date all the way back to Julius Caesar, Socrates, and many generations before them. Herbs are among the oldest and most reliable forms of medicine.

Practitioners who specialize in herbal remedies have a large storehouse of botanical remedies for the mind that enhance memory, concentration, and learning ability. Tinctures, teas, and herb-filled capsules are prescribed in different strengths and are tailored to each person's individual symptoms.

Ginkgo biloba, for instance, contains substances that enhance your cognitive abilities by increasing blood- and oxygen flow to the brain. Other herbs help you cope with memory-dampening physical and emotional stress, says Roy Upton, herbalist and director of the American Herbal Pharmacopeia in Santa Cruz, California. Often, the cause of your concentration problems is insomnia. In that case, you'll be given a remedy such as valerian to lull you to sleep.

To find a qualified herbalist in your area, contact the American Herbalists Guild, P.O. Box 70, Roosevelt, UT 84066. For more information on herbs, contact the Herb Research Foundation, 1007 Pearl Street, Suite 200, Boulder, CO 80302.

Hypnotists

Franz Anton Mesmer, the founder of modern hypnotism, mistakenly attributed its healing powers to "animal magnetism." But while his theory was less than magnetic, the general principles he espoused certainly have stuck.

A hypnotist can help you build your memory in two ways—either by increasing your self-esteem or by helping you rehearse tasks that require concentration. Studies show that hypnosis helps people pay attention, focus, and prioritize thoughts, according to psychologist Sam Migdole, Ed.D., secretary of the Board of Psychological Hypnosis in Beverly, Massachusetts.

People often have memory problems because they lack confidence or have overwhelming stress and anxiety, Dr. Migdole says. Using posthypnotic suggestion, a hypnotist can help you overcome fears by leading you through memory tasks you dread. While you're hypnotized, a hypnotist may suggest that you have a good memory or a superior ability to concentrate—and the posthypnotic effect is that you're able to remember things better even after you "wake up."

Long ago, perhaps, hypnotists used a swinging watch and the murmured suggestion, "You are getting sleepy" to induce hypnosis. But in today's clinical setting, most people are hypnotized simply by sitting in a comfortable chair and listening to the hypnotist's calming voice, Dr. Migdole says. He recommends that his patients bolster the effects of hypnosis by practicing it at home using the techniques he teaches them. Self-hypnosis involves breathing slowly and deeply, relaxing your body, and thinking about the goal you want to achieve, such as remembering certain facts. "Hypnosis often enhances sleep and relaxation, which helps to improve brain power too," says Dr. Migdole.

To find a qualified hypnotist in your area, write to the American Society of Clinical Hypnosis, 33 West Grand Avenue, Suite 402, Chicago, IL 60610.

Meditation Teachers

Since the early 1970s, studies have documented the beneficial effects of meditation on everything from lowering cholesterol to increasing relaxation to enhancing memory and learning. Essentially, a meditation instructor will teach you skills to mentally and physically quiet your mind so that you can concentrate.

There are many different types of meditation. These include Eastern disciplines, such as Zen Buddhist and Hindu meditation, and Western traditions, such as Christian or Jewish religious meditation combined with prayer.

An instructor can help you achieve a state of deep rest during meditation. Studies show that this deep rest lowers blood pressure, relaxes muscles, and decreases the secretion of stress hormones. Because meditation also increases your powers of concentration, the result is clearer thinking and more organized thoughts.

"A good meditation teacher is like a spiritual friend or coach," explains Victor Davich, author of *The Best Guide to Meditation*, who has conducted numerous meditation seminars during his 25 years as a practitioner.

When considering a potential teacher, ask about her training, methods of teaching, and fees. If possible, attend a class or retreat with the teacher before hiring her as your regular coach, suggests Davich.

Some meditation teachers will teach you how to sit quietly and focus on repeating a mantra—a word that becomes the object, or anchor, of your attention. Other meditation teachers may help you concentrate just on your breath or even on a spiritual riddle.

For information about meditation teachers, write to the Insight Meditation Society, 1230 Pleasant Street, Barre, MA 01005.

Oriental Medicine Specialists

Oriental medicine practitioners use a variety of tactics to increase your brain power, including Chinese herbs, acupuncture, and acupressure. They consider memory problems to be the result of imbalances that occur in heart and kidney energies.

"Heart energy rejuvenates your spirit. And kidney energy regulates the bone marrow, spine, and brain. So they're both important in enhancing memory," says David Molony, L.Ac., executive director of the American Association of Oriental Medicine in Catasauqua, Pennsylvania.

In Traditional Chinese Medicine, the body's 12 intersecting energetic meridians are thought to regulate the body energy known as *chi* (pronounced "chee"), and often correlate to different organs of the body. To enhance memory abilities, Oriental medicine practitioners insert hair-thin acupuncture needles or apply hand pressure (acupressure) at points on the meridians that are believed to increase kidney and heart energies.

A doctor trained in Oriental medicine may also prescribe individualized herbal mixtures that can be taken as powders, granules, or teas, Molony says. When mixing herbs, Chinese medical practitioners usually begin with patented formulas and then adjust these formulas for your individual needs.

An Oriental medicine practitioner also may advise you to practice meditation and the gentle martial art of tai chi. In addition, he might recommend home remedies, such as facials or scalp massages before bed, because these treatments help keep blood moving to the brain.

To find a qualified Oriental medicine practitioner in your area, contact the American Association of Oriental Medicine, 433 Front Street, Catasauqua, PA 18032.

For more information on these and other alternative healing modalities, contact the Office of Alternative Medicine (OAM) at the National Institute of Health (NIH). Write for their "General Information Package" at OAM Clearinghouse, P.O. Box 8218, Silver Spring, MD 20907.

Index